CASE STUDIES IN PREPARATION FOR THE CALIFORNIA READING COMPETENCY TEST

SECOND EDITION

JOANNE ROSSI
NOTRE DAME DE NAMUR UNIVERSITY, BELMONT

BETH SCHIPPER
CALIFORNIA STATE UNIVERSITY, FULLERTON

Boston   New York   San Francisco
Mexico City   Montreal   Toronto   London   Madrid   Munich   Paris
Hong Kong   Singapore   Tokyo   Cape Town   Sydney

Series Editor: *Aurora Martinez*
Editorial Assitant: *Beth Slater*
Production Administrator: *Paul Mihailidis*
Manufacturing Buyer: *Joanne Sweeney*
Cover Administrator: *Kristina Mose-Libon*

ISBN 0-205-36015-7

Printed in the United States of America

10 9 8 7 6 5 4 3 2 1   08 07 06 05 04 03 02

TABLE OF CONTENTS

Messages to our readers:

The book is designed to serve three audiences:

1. The preservice teacher/credential candidate
2. The college teacher of reading courses
3. The inservice teacher in the classroom

To the preservice teacher:

The purpose of this book is to provide practice in synthesizing and analyzing assessment and strategies for reading in K-8 classrooms. It is also designed to help you pass the Reading Initiative Competence Assessment (RICA™) administered by the state of California. While the case studies should aid your study for the RICA™, our hope is that the book will also enhance your assessment and instruction skills and, as a result, increase your students' learning.

The book is organized into a set of case studies for each grade level, followed by a format to assist you in brainstorming your knowledge before writing your response in narrative form. Following each brainstorming section are strategic ideas that you should have covered in writing your plan, as well as a sample narrative. At the end of the book is a bibliography of accessible and reader-friendly texts and other resources that can help you fill any gaps in your knowledge base.

To the college instructor:

These case studies are intended to aid students in their preparation for the RICA™, but the studies can also be used to enhance instruction in your reading courses, to foster analysis and discussions, to assist in-class problem-solving, and to assess student knowledge. The information from your assessment can assist you in planning your own instruction and, in turn, increase student learning in the elementary classrooms. The bibliography can provide resources for filling in gaps in student knowledge. The case studies represent all elementary grade levels, the four domains required by the RICA™ and a full range of instructional strategies. The studies are a compilation of actual profiles of readers in public and private schools in northern, central, and southern California. They also represent a wide diversity of cultures, levels, and skills.

To the inservice teacher in the classroom:

Given the diversity of the elementary classroom, the problems that classroom teachers face, as well as the increased accountability for student success, these case studies can help illuminate the problems and suggest strategies to improve student learning. They also should help you identify the gaps in your own knowledge and give you sources to further assist you in filling those gaps.

HOW TO USE THIS BOOK

Case Studies: Each Domain presents three case studies dealing with classes, small groups or individuals. We suggest that you **read what the Domain includes**, then **read the case study** and **make some notes** about what **strengths and needs** you perceive. Finally, note what **strategies you would** use for instruction along with the rationale for these strategies if the case study asks for it. For the cases that require assessment methods, **jot down some ideas** about the assessment tools you would use and why. Then you will be ready to **compare your ideas with the Response Ideas** we have listed on the pages that follow. (For most of the cases in this book, we have suggested more than one strategy; but **be prepared to discuss one strategy in-depth** in case the RICA asks you to focus on just one strategy). Once you are satisfied with your Response Ideas, you can write a narrative. Be advised that the RICA answer sheet gives you less space for cases in Domains I and IV and therefore, the narratives will be shorter. For cases in Domains II and III your narrative will be approximately half a page. For the large case study which covers Domains I-IV, you will have roughly a page for your narrative response (about 300 words).

Multiple Choice: Following the case studies for each of the Domains there are **multiple choice questions based on short scenarios**. The answers appear immediately after the questions. Use these to **test your knowledge of the content**, but also to **note any terms you may not know**. Put each of these terms on **index cards and study them over time**. There are references at the end of the book that you might consult to clarify a concept or you may wish to ask your instructor for an explanation. There is also a concept list after the bibliography.

ABOUT THE AUTHORS

Between them, the authors represent sixty years of experience in the field of reading and language arts as classroom teachers, reading specialists, curriculum consultants, clinicians, administrators, college teachers, and supervisors of student teachers. In the past twenty years, a major focus of their work has been in the research and instruction of language arts assessment in elementary and high school districts. They are also the authors of the book, *Portfolios in the Classrooms: Tools for Learning and Instruction.*

Reading Instruction Competency Assessment (RICA™): DOMAINS

Domain I:
Planning and Organizing Reading Instruction Based on Ongoing Assessment

Content Area 1: Conducting Ongoing Assessment of Reading Development
1.1 Principles of assessment
1.2 Assessing reading levels
1.3 Using and communicating assessment results

Content Area 2: Planning, Organizing, and Managing Reading Instruction
2.1 Factors involved in planning reading instruction
2.2 Organizing and managing reading instruction

Domain II:
Developing Phonological and Other Linguistic Processes Related to Reading

Content Area 3: Phonemic Awareness
3.1 Assessing phonemic awareness
3.2 The role of phonemic awareness
3.3 Developing phonemic awareness

Content Area 4: Concepts About Print
4.1 Assessing concepts about print
4.2 Concepts about print
4.3 Letter recognition

Content Area 5: Systematic, Explicit Phonics and Other Word Identification Strategies
5.1 Assessing phonics and other word identification strategies
5.2 Explicit phonics instruction
5.3 Developing fluency
5.4 Word identification strategies
5.5 Sight words
5.6 Terminology

Content Area 6: Spelling Instruction
6.1 Assessing spelling
6.2 Systematic spelling instruction
6.3 Spelling instruction in context

Domain III:
Developing Reading Comprehension and Promoting Independent Reading

Content Area 7: Reading Comprehension
7.1 Assessing reading comprehension
7.2 Fluency and other factors affecting comprehension
7.3 Facilitating comprehension
7.4 Different levels of comprehension
7.5 Comprehension strategies

Content Area 8: Literary Response and Analysis
8.1 Assessing literary response and analysis
8.2 Responding to literature
8.3 Literary analysis

Content Area 9: Content Area Literacy
9.1 Assessing content area literacy
9.2 Different types of texts and purposes for reading
9.3 Study skills

Content Area 10: Student Independent Reading
10.1 Encouraging independent reading
10.2 Supporting at-home reading

Domain IV:
Supporting Reading Through Oral and Written Language Development

Content Area 11: Relationships Among Reading, Writing, and Oral Language
11.1 Assessing oral and written language
11.2 Oral language development
11.3 Written language development
11.4 Supporting English language learners

Content Area 12: Vocabulary Development

12.1 Assessing vocabulary knowledge
12.2 Increasing vocabulary knowledge
12.3 Strategies for gaining and extending meanings of words

Content Area 13: Structure of the English Language

13.1 Assessing English language structures
13.2 Differences between written and oral English
13.3 Applying knowledge of the English language to improve reading

DOMAIN I

4th Grade Individual

Mitsy is a second semester fourth grader who is having difficulty in her class. Look at the attached test scores and reading sample. Determine the student's approximate instructional and independent reading levels. Briefly tell what information you would discuss with both the student and parent about this student's performance and what will be the main focus of your instructional plan.

Scores from a standard test:

	Percentile	Grade Equivalent
Word Attack	45th	4.0
Reading Vocabulary	75th	5.2
Passage Comprehension	23rd	3.2
Literal	48th	4.2
Inference	20th	3.0
Critical Thinking	40th	3.9
Main Idea	25th	3.3

To determine a student's reading level using an informal reading inventory, use the following formula generally accepted:

	Word Recognition*	Comprehension
Independent Level	99% or higher	90% or higher
Instructional Level	90-95% or higher	60-80% or higher
Frustration Level	90% or lower	60% or lower
Listening Level		75-80% or higher

*Note: Not all errors result in loss of meaning, e.g., "the" for "a", "house" for "home", retain the meaning.

2

Mitsy

The Promise (4)

INTRODUCTION: This story is about two girls walking together. Please read to find out what happens to them.

The Promise

Long ago, in a distant land beside the sea, people often spotted mermaids. The mermaids had fantastic treasures.

Sometimes the mermaids would swim to shore. They would spread their treasures around them on the sand. If anyone came near, however, they would jump back in the sea.

One day, two little girls walking on a beach spied a mermaid. To their surprise, she did not swim away when she saw them. Instead, she smiled and called them over. She gave each a bundle of treasure. "Do not open them until you get home," she warned. The girls promised not to. Then off they went, happy and excited.

One girl soon grew impatient. When she was out of sight of the mermaid, she decided to open her gift. To her disappointment, she found only ashes and dust.

The other girl kept her promise. She did not look inside until she got home. In her bundle she found gold, silver, and sparkling jewels. Her family was delighted, and they never forgot their good fortune.

R = repeat
sc = self-correct

_____

dk = don't know

From Ezra L. Stieglitz. _The Stieglitz Informal Reading Inventory._ (Second Edition) Boston, Massachusetts: Allyn and Bacon 1997

COMPREHENSION CHECK

	Probed Recall	Free Recall
L 1. Where does this story take place? (by the sea) (on a beach)	___	✓
L 2. Who did the little girls see? (a mermaid)	___	✓
L 3. What did the mermaid give to each girl? (a bundle of treasure)	dk	___
L 4. What was the promise both girls made to the mermaid? (not to open their bundles of treasure until they got home)	___	✓
I 5. How did the girl who opened up the first bundle of treasure feel? (sad) (upset) (disappointed)	dk	___
C 6. What is the lesson we can learn from this story? (Accept any logical response, such as "If you keep your promise, many good things will come your way" or "Listen to people and heed their warnings.")	✓	_ _

Total Comprehension Errors ___2___
(L & I)

Retell

The mermaid gave the girls something. I don't know what it was called When they opened it they found different things.

MAKE SOME NOTES OF YOUR OWN BEFORE TURNING THE PAGE

Strengths:

Needs:

Strategies:

Response Ideas

Reading Sample:
- uses initial consonants and blends
- has some difficulty with endings
- guesses without using context clues
- uses some syntactical cues
- self-corrects at times
- repeats words and phrases
- gives a fair retelling
- her answers to questions reflect standardized test pattern

Strengths:
- major strength is in vocabulary
- from the standardized test — relative strengths are in word attack, answering literal questions (factual or detail questions), critical thinking (opinion, application)
- from the informal individual reading assessment — uses some graphophonemic, syntactic, and semantic cues
- does some self-correcting
- remembers some details

Needs:
- medial vowels and work on endings
- comprehension skills — reading for meaning (monitoring), consistency in using cue systems, synthesizing for main idea, inferential thinking (answering inference questions), elaboration in retelling
- fluency

Narrative:
Mitsy's independent level is approximately at the third grade; instructional level is high third, low fourth. Although she has basic reading strengths and is beginning to correct her mistakes, Misty will need to work on medial vowels and endings and some structural analysis skills. These skills will help to improve fluency. The instructional plan should focus on comprehension skills primarily, main idea, inferential thinking, and elaboration in retelling.

Domain I

2nd Grade Class

This second grade class is located in an affluent area near many large corporations. The parents volunteer in the classroom on a regular basis. Ninety percent of the parents show up for parent-teacher conferences, and they have high expectations for their children. With class size reduction, there are twentey students in the class. It is the first week of school. You need to get to know the strengths and needs of your students in order to plan instruction. What kinds of assessment tools and strategies will you use, and what is your rationale for your choices?

MAKE SOME NOTES OF YOUR OWN BEFORE TURNING THE PAGE

Types of Assessment Tools and Strategies:

Rationale:

Response Ideas

Types of Assessment Tools and Strategies:

- informal reading inventories, running records (Clay, 1979), miscue analysis and retellings (Goodman and Burke, 1970) on audio tapes
- observations using checklists for listening, speaking, reading, and writing behaviors
- anecdotal records
- writing samples
- student interest and strategy inventory
- student-teacher conferences
- portfolios (include work from first grade, if possible)

Rationale:

- assessments listed are based on data about individual strengths and needs
- span all language arts areas — reading, writing, listening, speaking
- allow teacher to interact with students on an individual basis
- allow teacher to see patterns in order to group students
- performance based in real reading, writing, listening, and speaking situations
- baseline data provides starting point to show evidence of growth over time
- ongoing assessment uses multiple measures

Narrative:

The teacher may get baseline information by doing the following individual assessments: readings and retellings on audio tapes, observations, checklists, anecdotal records, writing samples, student inventory, student-teacher conferences, and portfolios. Assessments provide data about individual strengths and needs; they allow instructional planning for grouping students at different levels; ongoing assessment shows growth over time which can be communicated to parents.

Domain I

7th Grade Class

This class has thirty students from mixed backgrounds and cultures: five Chinese, seven Filipino, ten African-American, and eight Caucasians. The school is located in an urban setting, and some students are bused to the school. Only 25 percent of the students in this class are English Language Learners. What kinds of assessments will you use and how will you use the results?

MAKE SOME NOTES OF YOUR OWN BEFORE TURNING THE PAGE

Assessment Strategies:

Use of the Results:

Response Ideas

Assessment Strategies:
- observation and anecdotal records
- reading analysis with retelling(miscue analysis (Goodman and Burke, 1970), running records (Clay, 1979), informal reading inventories)
- conferences with students and parents to talk about strengths, needs, interests, culture, etc.
- portfolios

Use of the Results:
- gathering of baseline data
- ongoing assessment to inform instruction — informal and standardized
- grouping according to instructional level
- grouping according to specific skills
- whole class instruction
- differentiated individualized instruction according to individual needs
- chose materials depending on the independent and instructional levels of the students

Narrative:
In order to plan instruction (group, whole class, and individualized), select materials, and inform both students and parents. Extensive assessment, both informal and standardized, should be done on an ongoing basis. Use observations, checklists, keep anecdotal records, give reading analyses with retelling, hold conferences, and use portfolios to show growth in reading and writing over time.

Multiple Choice – Domain I

Question 1:

Ms. Nguyen believes that she has developed a balanced, comprehensive reading/language arts program for her third graders. She includes instruction in all four language arts – reading, writing, listening and speaking, a mix of skills in decoding, strategies in comprehension, and literature-based instruction. What major component is missing that would allow her to better inform her instruction and meet the needs of all learners:
   a)   scaffolding
   b)   visual aids
   c)   oral language development
   d)   assessment

Question 2:

Mrs. Gomez does an informal reading inventory on each of her students in her seventh grade language arts core class. What information is she not likely to glean from this assessment:
   a)   information about the student's attitude toward reading
   b)   information about what decoding and word analysis strategies the student is using
   c)   information about whether the student is monitoring for understanding while reading
   d)   information about the student's ability to answer questions about the text

Question 3:

After Mrs. Gomez does the evaluation of the inventory, she discusses the results with each of the students. What is the main reason for this practice:
   a)   to correct their word pronunciations
   b)   to allow them to communicate the information to their parents
   c)   to show them where they are weak
   d)   to make them partners in their reading instruction

Question 4:

Mrs. Gomez also administers a standardized reading test to her students. She needs to interpret the results and communicate them to the parents. The results are reported in percentiles. Max's score fell into the 65th percentile for total reading. When Max's parents ask what a percentile is, how would she define it and explain Max's percentile score to his parents:

    a)   Max is a below average reader
    b)   Max reads better than 65 percent of the students in seventh grade classes
    c)   Max has poor strategies for comprehension
    d)   Max's score would be equal to a C or a D on a his report card

Question 5:

Mrs. Fari has a new kindergarten and needs to obtain some baseline data on her students. One of the assessments will deal with concepts about print. Which of the following would not be included in this particular assessment:

    a)   left-to-right orientation
    b)   cover of the book
    c)   word segmentation
    d)   recognition of a capital letter

Answers for Domain I

Question 1:

d) assessment because without it she will have a difficult time matching the needs of the individual students and the whole group with the instruction that would best serve those needs. Answers a) and b) are comprehension strategies; oral language development is already embedded under the umbrella of listening and speaking in the category of language arts.

Question 2:

a) information about the student's attitude toward reading. Although the teacher may have a discussion about the student's attitude toward reading, this information is not automatically embedded in the IRI procedure. All of the other answers contain components of an analysis of student reading behaviors that could be gleaned from an IRI.

Question 3:

d) to make them partners in their reading instruction. In order for students to be engaged in reading and empower them to make progress, they need to understand what strategies good readers use that they are already using, and then what kinds of skills and strategies they need to work on in collaboration with their teacher. Answer a) is not part of this process. Answer b) may happen, but it is not the main reason the teacher holds the conference. Answer c) is only a part of the process, but not the main reason for the conference.

Question 4:

b) Max reads better than 65 percent of the students in seventh grade classes. Answer a) is incorrect because the score tells that Max is an above average reader. Answer c) is incorrect because we would need more data to confirm this, and it is unlikely given his percentile score. Answer d) is also unlikely, and even though a student's percentile score might reflect his performance in the classroom, we do not use standardized tests to determine a student's grade on a report card.

Question 5:

c) word segmentation which is a component of phonemic awareness, not concepts about print. The other answers are concepts about print that include going from left to right, identifying the cover of the book, and the recognition of a capital letter.

DOMAIN II

2nd Grade Individual

Carmen is a second grade non-English speaker (NEP). She attends an ESL class for an hour each day. In her regular classroom, she tends to be shy but will risk giving some answers. When she is around one other child who also speaks Spanish but has more control of English (Limited English Proficiency or LEP), Carmen is bubbly, outgoing and can carry on a conversation in her native language with ease. When speaking in the ESL class she can use some basic English. Carmen has some concepts of print and some knowledge of the alphabet. She was unable to attempt a phonemic awareness test in English. She is able to write her name and draw a simple picture of a person. On the following page there are some sample assessments from Carmen. Together with this background and the assessments, tell what kinds of strategies you would use with Carmen and why you think these strategies would be effective.

Checklist for Observing Concepts about Print

NAME												
Carmen					;							
Time at school	24rs.											
Front of book	—											
Print contains message	✓											
Where to start	✓											
Left to right	✓											
Return sweep	✓											
Word by word matching	✓											
First and last	✓											
Print is right way up	✓											
Left page before right	✓											
Full stop	—											
Question mark	—											
Capital and lower case letter correspondence	—											
Letters	✓											
Recognizes difference/ knows the term.												
Words	—											
First and last letters of words	—											
Capital letters	—											
Comments												

This page is copyright-free

Legend
✓ knows
0 does not know
— does not know
0✓ corrected by student

Table 5.1 **Alphabet Recognition Test** *Carmen*

A S D F (G) H (J)
(K) (L) (P) O I (U) (Y)
T R E (W) Q Z X
(C) (V) B (N) (M)

a s d f (g) h j
(k) l p o i u (y)
t (r) (e) (w) (q) (z) x
c (v) b n m a (y)
(g) q t a (g) t (q)

From Margaret Ann Richek, et al. *Reading Problems: Assessment and Teaching Strategies* (Third Edition). Needham, Massachusetts: Allyn and Bacon, 1996

MAKE SOME NOTES OF YOUR OWN BEFORE TURNING THE PAGE

Strengths:

Needs:

Strategies and Rationale:

Response Ideas

Strengths:

- is verbal in Spanish, her native language
- is an emergent reader
- has some concepts of print in place
- knows some alphabet letters
- can communicate at basic English level
- is able to draw a simple picture of a person
- is able to write her name
- has some good social skills

Needs:

- English language development (vocabulary and syntax)
- beginning reading instruction — phonemic awareness, additional concepts of print, sight words, systematic phonics, spelling patterns
- immersion in environmental print

Strategies and Rationale:

- additional practice with phonemic awareness — poems, rhymes, chants, choral reading, alphabet in different contexts — preparation for phonics
- systematic phonics — beginning consonants, long and short vowels, blends, onsets and rimes — basic strategies for decoding
- predictable books and decodable text — reading text which reinforces skills
- sound blending with cross-checking — trying out various letter sounds, blending them together until the result is a word that makes sense — monitoring strategy
- language experience approach using stories dictated by the student so that she can connect what she is saying with written text
- oral cloze (Taylor, 1953; Meeks & Morgan, 1978) — read-alouds in the context of shared reading (Holdaway, 1979; Lynch, 1986) with certain words supplied by the student — develops use of context clues
- spelling practice with consonant-vowel-consonant (cvc) pattern and beyond (e.g., cvce), journal writing, dictation, word wall, individual dictionary — application of phonics and independence in writing
- teacher read-alouds of quality literature which include helping student make pre-dictions and listening to check predictions — helps model pronunciation and reading process
- daily independent reading — promotes fluency and positive attitude toward reading

Narrative:

Carmen is an emergent reader in a school with a program that emphasizes learning English. Therefore, the teacher should model syntax of the English language and new vocabulary through read-alouds. Carmen needs phonemic awareness instruction (e.g., through poems, rhymes), immersion in and concepts of print (e.g., letter recognition), and systematic phonics, which all will lay the groundwork for beginning reading strategies and skills. Carmen should be reading daily, especially predictable books, and decodable text to practice the application of skills. Practice with writing and spelling will allow her to practice phonetic skills and English syntax. Her ability to take some risks will help her to dictate text and read her own words and thus connect speech with print and promote fluency.

DOMAIN II

3rd Grade Group

This particular class has a high percentage of students in Title I. For the most part, they are all English speaking. Few of the children are read to at home but all enjoy story time when the teacher reads to them. They also enjoy independent reading when they get to look at or read a book by themselves. Four of the students are in the emergent reader stage, a beginning first grade level. They have some sight words under control, they read word-by-word and therefore, reading is laborious. Reading and phonics analysis shows that they know most initial consonant sounds and use those to randomly guess at the word, but they ignore ending consonants and medial vowels. Both writing and spelling are on a lower developmental level: beginning of first grade, phonetic stage. What instruction would you provide for this group and what supported your choices?

MAKE SOME NOTES OF YOUR OWN BEFORE TURNING THE PAGE

Strengths:

Needs:

Strategies:

Response Ideas

Strengths:
- have some sight words under control
- know most consonant sounds
- have an interest in reading
- have some comprehension of what they are reading

Needs:
- phonics skills on an automatic level to promote fluency and comfort with reading
- strategies to retain sight words
- strategies for monitoring and self-correction
- strategies for spelling

Strategies:
- give opportunities to apply phonics skills using contexts such as decodable or predictable texts during shared reading
- based on needs, do direct and systematic instruction in phonics with emphasis on phonemes, e.g., onsets and rimes, blends, vowels, digraphs, syllables
- create activity centers that provide practice in phonics skills and previously taught generalizations
- have direct instruction in strategies for monitoring and self-correction in reading, e.g., using picture and context clues to support graphophonemic elements
- language experience approach with follow-up mini-lessons on word patterns that present difficulties
- choral reading to promote word recognition and fluency
- add think-alouds (Nist & Kirby, 1986; Randall, Fairbanks & Kennedy, 1986) to read-alouds where teacher models how good readers process text as they read
- send books home that students have practiced and have them share them with their parents; this will encourage home or family literacy involvement
- provide opportunities for writing authentic pieces every day (authentic reflects writing that is purposeful and meaningful)
- provide opportunities for interactive writing (McKenzie, 1986) with students and teacher (shared pen, shared writing)

- put up word walls that contain the most frequently used words; students need to add to the wall and refer to it when writing
- have individual, student-made dictionaries
- provide word cards that contain the words that the individual is struggling with; student needs to review cards each day and practice using visual, auditory, tactile, and kinesthetic modes so that the student sees the word, listens to the sounds in the word, writes the word and then traces each letter with a finger to get the "feel" of the word using different modalities
- conduct individual reading and writing conferences with the teacher to nurture strengths and support weak areas

Narrative:

By third grade, if this group has had a continuous phonics program from the beginning of school, instruction should include the language experience approach with follow-up mini-lessons on word patterns that present difficulties. Based on needs, do direct and systematic instruction in phonics with emphasis on phonemes; give ample opportunities to apply phonics skills using contexts such as decodable or predictable texts; create activity centers that provide practice in phonics skills and previously taught generalizations; and have direct instruction in strategies for monitoring and self-correction in reading, (e.g., using picture and context clues to support graphophonemic elements). In addition, provide choral readings to promote word recognition and fluency; add think-alouds to read-alouds; send books home to share with parents; provide opportunities for writing authentic pieces every day; encourage interactive writing; use word walls, student-made dictionaries and word cards; practice words using different learning modes; and conduct individual reading and writing conferences to nurture strengths and support weak areas.

DOMAIN II

1st Grade Group

In this first grade class there are various Asian languages and cultures represented. They are all second generation and English proficient. It is November of the year and many of the students can read simple, decodable text that follows predictable patterns with high frequency sight words. However, four of the students are non-readers and writers. They are reluctant to take any risks in either speaking or writing. What assessment strategies should this teacher employ to determine her plan of instruction for these students and why would she use these particular methods?

MAKE SOME NOTES OF YOUR OWN BEFORE TURNING THE PAGE

Types of Assessments & Rationale:

Response Ideas

Types of Assessments & Rationale:

- concepts about print (Clay, 1993) — shows book handling, left-to-right orientation and top and bottom (directionality), upper and lower case letter recognition, one-to-one letter and word correspondence, tracking, realization that print is speech written down, knowledge of punctuation and capitalization
- phonemic awareness test - (the stage prior to phonics instruction) a verbal assessment that tests students' knowledge that words are made up of individual sounds (phonemes), that they are able to blend sounds together to make syllables and words (sound blending), are able to break words down (segmention),and make substitutions and deletions using onsets and rimes
- listening samples with retelling to assess students' ability to remember, understand, and sequence a story
- observations and anecdotal records to detail and document benchmarks and developmental milestones in listening and speaking
- sight word assessment to see whether students have visual memory for sight vocabulary (high-frequency words)
- individual conferences to find out about family literacy history, such as whether students were read to at home, what language is spoken by parents, whether parents are readers, how much TV students watch, students' interests, the extent of their outside activities (e.g., Asian language instruction, ballet, music, soccer, and art classes)

Narrative:

The following measures will yield information about a student's readiness to read: 1) a "concepts of print" test that shows book handling, directionality, upper and lower case letter recognition, one-to-one letter and word correspondence, tracking, realization that print is speech written down and knowledge of punctuation and capitalization; 2) a "phonemic awareness" test to determine whether students know that words are made up of phonemes, that they are able to blend or segment sounds, and make substitutions and deletions using onsets and rimes; 3) listening samples with retelling to assess students' ability to remember, understand and sequence a story; 4) observations and anecdotal records to detail and document benchmarks and developmental milestones in listening and speaking; 4) sight word assessment to see whether students have visual memory for sight vocabulary (high-frequency words); and 5) individual conferences to find out about family literacy history such as whether students were read to at home, and other factors related to reading.

DOMAIN II

Kindergarten Class

In this first semester Kindergarten class there are twenty students. 25 percent have Spanish as their first language, and 25 percent have Tagalog as their primary language (eight have limited English and two are non English speaking). The other 50 percent are English speaking. There is a mixture of socioeconomic levels; many are bused in from outlying rural areas. Two-thirds of the students have had no preschool experiences. Discuss what kinds of strengths most of the representative samples on the next four pages reveal, and name three major prereading instructional methods you would use with this class.

Checklist for Observing Concepts about Print

NAME

Minna L.

Time at school	Big										
Front of book	✓										
Print contains message	—										
Where to start	—										
Left to right	—										
Return sweep	—										
Word by word matching	—										
First and last	—										
Print is right way up	—										
Left page before right	—										
Full stop	—										
Question mark	—										
Capital and lower case letter correspondence	—										
Letters	✓—										
Recognizes difference/ knows the term.											
Words											
First and last letters of words	—										
Capital letters	—										
Comments											

This page is copyright-free

Knows a few letters.
(all Capitals)

Minna L.

Listening & Speaking Asset Sheet

Name Minna L. Grade K Year 199—

(circle) NEP LEP ESL

	1st Date	2nd Date
Comprehension		
Can tell the difference		
between words	✓	
Gains understanding		
when spoken to	✓	
when read to	✓—	
Can hold information in memory	✓—	
Is able to follow directions		
one step	✓	
two step	—	
three or more steps	—	
Expression		
Speaks clearly	✓—	
Uses language appropriately		
in social situations	✓—	
Uses vocabulary appropriate to age		
in classroom	✓—	
Uses standard English grammar	—	
Uses standard native language	✓	
Can retell a story	—	
in sequence		
with major details		
Can label and categorize		
things	—	
ideas		
Communicates meaningful ideas	✓—	
Participates in discussions	✓—	
Responses to questions		
in organized manner		
on factual level		
on inferential level		
on critical thinking level		
Uses language to solve problems		

© Joanne Rossi & Beth Schipper, 1994

Checklist for Observing Concepts about Print

NAME *Benny D.*

	Beg.							
Time at school	Beg.							
Front of book	✓							
Print contains message	✓							
Where to start	✓							
Left to right	—							
Return sweep	—							
Word by word matching	—							
First and last	—							
Print is right way up	—							
Left page before right	✓							
Full stop	—							
Question mark	—							
Capital and lower case letter correspondence	—							
Letters	✓							
Recognizes difference								
knows the term.								
Words	—							
First and last letters of words	—							
Capital letters	—							
Comments								

This page is copyright-free

Can recognize most letters – upper and lower c...

Listening & Speaking Asset Sheet

Name *Benny D.*   Grade *K* Year *199—*

(circle)   NEP LEP (ESL)

Comprehension	1st Date	2nd Date
Can tell the difference		
between words	✓	___
Gains understanding		
when spoken to	✓	___
when read to	✓	___
Can hold information in memory	✓	___
Is able to follow directions		
one step	✓	___
two step	✓	___
three or more steps	—	___
Expression		
Speaks clearly	✓–	___
Uses language appropriately		
in social situations	✓–	___
Uses vocabulary appropriate to age		
in classroom	✓–	___
Uses standard English grammar	✓–	___
Uses standard native language	✓	___
Can retell a story	✓	___
in sequence	✓	___
with major details	✓	___
Can label and categorize		
things	✓	___
ideas		___
Communicates meaningful ideas	✓–	___
Participates in discussions	✓–	___
Responses to questions		
in organized manner		___
on factual level	✓	___
on inferential level	___	___
on critical thinking level	___	___
Uses language to solve problems	___	___

Joanne Rossi & Beth Schipper, 1994

B

August

Benny D.

Checklist for Observing Concepts about Print

NAME
Alviar F.

Time at school	Beg.
Front of book	✓
Print contains message	—
Where to start	
Left to right	—
Return sweep	—
Word by word matching	—
First and last	—
Print is right way up	—
Left page before right	—
Full stop	—
Question mark	
Capital and lower case letter correspondence	—
Letters	
Recognizes difference/	
knows the term.	
Words	—
First and last letters of words	—
Capital letters	—
Comments	

This page is copyright-free

Cannot recognize letters by name yet.

August

Alviar F.

Listening & Speaking Asset Sheet

Name **Alviar F.** Grade **K** Year **199—**
(circle) NEP (LEP) ESL

	1st Date	2nd Date
Comprehension		
Can tell the difference		
between words	✓–	___
Gains understanding		
when spoken to	✓	___
when read to	✓	___
Can hold information in memory	—	___
Is able to follow directions		
one step	—	___
two step		___
three or more steps		___
Expression		
Speaks clearly	✓–	___
Uses language appropriately		
in social situations	✓–	___
Uses vocabulary appropriate to age		
in classroom	✓–	___
Uses standard English grammar	–	___
Uses standard native language	✓	___
Can retell a story	–	___
in sequence	—	___
with major details	—	___
Can label and categorize		
things	—	___
ideas	–	___
Communicates meaningful ideas	–	___
Participates in discussions	✓–	___
Responses to questions		
in organized manner		___
on factual level	✓–	___
on inferential level		___
on critical thinking level		___
Uses language to solve problems		___

© Joanne Rossi & Beth Schipper, 1994

Checklist for Observing Concepts about Print

NAME

Rena P.

Time at school	Beg						
Front of book	✓						
Print contains message	✓						
Where to start	—						
Left to right	—						
Return sweep	—						
Word by word matching	—						
First and last	—						
Print is right way up	—						
Left page before right	—						
Full stop	—						
Question mark	—						
Capital and lower case letter correspondence	—						
Letters							
Recognizes difference/ knows the term.							
Words							
First and last letters of words	—						
Capital letters	—						
Comments	—						

This page is copyright-free

Knows about 10 letters – upper case

Listening & Speaking Asset Sheet

Name *Rena P.* Grade *K* Year *199–*

(circle) NEP LEP (ESL)

	1st Date	2nd Date
Comprehension		
Can tell the difference		
between words	✓	
Gains understanding		
when spoken to	✓	
when read to	✓	
Can hold information in memory	—	
Is able to follow directions		
one step	✓	
two step	✓	
three or more steps		
Expression		
Speaks clearly	✓	
Uses language appropriately		
in social situations	✓–	
Uses vocabulary appropriate to age		
in classroom	✓–	
Uses standard English grammar	✓–	
Uses standard native language	✓	
Can retell a story	—	
in sequence	—	
with major details	—	
Can label and categorize		
things	✓	
ideas	—	
Communicates meaningful ideas	✓	
Participates in discussions	✓	
Responses to questions		
in organized manner		
on factual level	✓	
on inferential level	—	
on critical thinking level	—	
Uses language to solve problems	—	

August

Rena P.

MAKE SOME NOTES OF YOUR OWN BEFORE TURNING THE PAGE

Strengths:

Needs:

Strategies:

Response Ideas

Strengths:

◆ most students have some knowledge of English syntax
◆ most students can follow simple, one step directions
◆ most can speak in full sentences
◆ most can draw recognizable shapes
◆ most can retell some details from listening to a story
◆ most can answer simple questions

Needs:

◆ groundwork for reading, including phonemic awareness, letter and letter-sound recognition, structure of text (words and sentences), immersion in print, concepts about print

Strategies:

◆ teach concepts of print using read-alongs with predictable text (text with repetitive patterns), model directionality (the left-to-right orientation of text), word-by-word matching, tracking across the page, stopping at the ends of sentences
◆ immerse the classroom environment in print; label corners of the room and objects around the room; practice daily messages, (days of the week, months of the year, weather for the day, events at school, etc.)
◆ give students practice activities that involve visual recognition of shapes and names of alphabet letters through various hands-on activities (tactile/kinesthetic), such as, magnetic letters, felt boards, games, etc.
◆ practice the sounds of word patterns through chanting, choral reading, rhymes in poetry
◆ practice oral cloze (during choral reading, stop just before a word and ask class to tell what the next word will be; in the beginning of this activity, use words with rhyming pattern) (Taylor, 1953; Meeks & Morgan, 1978); this activity shows students that print has meaning

Narrative:

From the work samples it appears that most students: have some knowledge of English syntax, can follow simple, one step directions, speak in full sentences, draw recognizable shapes, retell some details from listening to a story, and most can answer simple questions. They will need to extend their concepts about print (directionality, word-by-word matching, tracking, etc.) through read-alongs using predictable text. They will need a classroom immersed in print: corners of the room and objects around the room labeled; and practice with daily messages, (days of the week, months of the year, weather for the day, events at school, etc.). Students will also need practice in the visual recognition of shapes and names of alphabet letters through various hands-on activities (tactile/kinesthetic), such as, magnetic letters, felt boards, games, etc. They can practice the sounds of word patterns through chanting, choral reading, and rhymes. Also, to show that print has meaning, they should practice oral cloze during choral reading.

Multiple Choice – Domain II

Question 1:

One of Mrs. Watkins's second grade reading groups has some difficulty applying phonics strategies. Out of the following phonics generalizations/rules/components, which one would be the least useful for her to focus on:

    a)   the *r*-controlled vowel
    b)   the *ch* as it is pronounced in *kitchen*
    c)   *gh* is silent as it is in *night*
    d)   the phonogram *ie* as it is in *field*

Question 2:

In his kindergarten class Mr. Gonzales has many students who are not yet readers. Using this information, answer the following questions:

Mr. Gonzales is reading an example of predictable text. Which of the following is an example of what he might be reading:

    a)   Once upon a time, a troll wandered the woods in search of gold.
    b)   Brown Bear, Brown Bear, what do you see?
    c)   Pat has a cat that sits on the mat.
    d)   There was an old woman who lived in a shoe; she had so many children she didn't know what to do.

Question 3:

Which of the following phonemic awareness activities is considered to be the lowest level of difficulty:

    a)   segmentation
    b)   blending
    c)   rhyming
    d)   substitutions/additions/deletions

Question 4:

In addition to teaching phonemic awareness activities, Mr. Gonzales is going to intro-
duce letter and sound recognition. This would be the beginning of:
- a)   onsets and rimes
- b)   blends
- c)   alphabetic principle
- d)   Elkonin boxes

Question 5:

In her first grade class Ms. Haddad used sentence strips in a pocket chart to present the
verse "Peter Piper picked a peck of pickled peppers," which she had the students chant.
She then asked the students to tell what they noticed about the sentence. This is an
example of what type of instruction:
- a)   differentiated instruction
- b)   implicit or embedded phonics
- c)   explicit, systematic phonics
- d)   structural analysis

Question 6:

On another day, Ms. Haddad used Lesson 5 from the Teacher's Manual to reinforce the
"p" in the initial consonant position. First, she told the students that they would be work-
ing on the letter "p." She showed them the letter "p" on a card and discussed what sound
it makes in the initial position. Students had a slate board and chalk. They divided their
slate into four sections, each section containing a word family (rime) such as _ot,_at,
_ill, _al. Ms. Haddad said the word "pat" and the students filled in the initial consonant
in the blank space. She then asked the students to hold up their slates to check their
work. This is an example of what type of instruction:
- a)   explicit, systematic phonics
- b)   implicit, embedded phonics
- c)   structural analysis
- d)   differentiated instruction

Question 7:

Mrs. Lee has a fifth grade group she has assessed with fluency problems. Which of the following would not be an effective strategy for Mrs. Lee to use to increase their fluency:
   a)   having the students point to each word as they read
   b)   having them do repeated readings of the same text
   c)   increase speed of word recognition
   d)   daily independent reading time (SSR, DEAR)

Question 8:

Mrs. Lee has another group that needs work in structural analysis. Which of the following words would best lend itself to this skill:
   a)   preconceived
   b)   laugh
   c)   mountains
   d)   decided

Question 9:

In her Writer's Workshop Mrs. Lee noticed that students needed work on spelling. Which of the following strategies would be the least effective in supporting students in spelling:
   a)   using the dictionary
   b)   word walls
   c)   frequent practice in writing and proofreading
   d)   class spelling tests

Answers for Domain II

Question 1

d) since this a phonics rule that has the most exceptions to its rule (17 percent utility). The other generalizations/rules have much higher percentages of usefulness or utility: Answer a) the *r-controlled* vowel has 78 percent utility; b) the *k* sound of has 95 percent utility; and c) the silent *gh* has 100 percent utility. (Source Clymer, 1963)

Question 2:

b) "Brown Bear, Brown Bear, what do you see?" because its text contains a predictable pattern that students will be able to recognize and reproduce with practice. Answer a) might give students a sense of story since many stories begin with "Once upon a time," but students don't automatically know what will come next in the story. Answer c) is decodable text, one that follows a decodable pattern, in this case, *at*. Answer d) is incorrect because although it contains rhyme, students cannot automatically predict the next line.

Question 3:

c) rhyming. According to the progression of difficulty in phonemic awareness, students generally have less difficulty with rhyming than they do with b) making a word out of its phonemes (*p-a-t = pat*), a) breaking a word down into its phonemes (*pat=p-a-t*), or d) making new words by substituting letters (taking away p from pat and adding b to make bat).

Question 4:

c) the alphabetic principle where students learn letter-sound association. Answers a) and b) are components of this principle. Answer d) is a strategy teachers might use to demonstrate single phonemes, blends or digraphs.

Question 5:

b) implicit or embedded phonics. This occurs when the teacher uses the phonetic pattern of the text to teach a lesson on phonics and asks the students to find the pattern, in this case the consonant *p* in the initial position of a word. Answer a) does not apply because there is no evidence that these students were singled out to have this lesson. Answer c) is incorrect because this lesson was created using a sentence in which the phonetic component was a part; explicit instruction would have begun with the presentation of the phonetic component in the beginning of the lesson. Answer d) has to do with multisyllabic words that lend themselves to an analysis of their roots, suffixes, prefixes, origin, etc.

Question 6:

a) this is an example of a teacher presenting the phonic concept first and giving the students guided practice. The explanations for Question 5 apply here as well.

Question 7:

a) because by the time students are in the fifth grade they need to have "ditched the finger" and stopped pointing to each word. This practice actually retards fluency. The other strategies all enhance speed and fluency: by helping readers to recognize words more quickly they increase automaticity c), by having them do repeated readings b) they will be able to experience what fluency "feels" like, and d) by reading daily and using books at their independent level they can only get better at reading and fluency.

Question 8:

a) preconceived. It is the only word out of the choices that contains a prefix (pre), and a root (conceive). Structural analysis deals with these components.

Question 9:

d) class spelling tests. Research has found these to be the least effective because many students may pass the tests but not generalize to their own writing. The other methods all support both authentic practice and ways in which to build independence in spelling.

DOMAIN III

3rd Grade Class

This is a third grade classroom in a middle class neighborhood. The student-teacher ratio is 20:1. Half of the class is African American; the other half is Caucasian. There is a high level of parent involvement — parents volunteer in the class, they raise money for materials and additional services (such as a full-time librarian), they read to their children at home, etc. The students have a high level of oral language and vocabulary. They also have good sight vocabulary and strong decoding skills due to a systematic phonics program in the first grade. However, the teacher notes that many students put words in sentences that don't make sense and they rarely self-correct. They also have difficulty answering open-ended questions and supporting and expanding their answers. Given this information and the dialogues below, decide what instructional strategies you would use. Include a rationale for your choices.

Dialogue 1:

Teacher: (having heard one student read aloud) Hmm. I'm confused by something you just read, Paul. You said "All of a sudden a *house* came galloping down the street." I have a certain picture in my mind when you read this sentence, but it's a very strange sight. Does that make sense in this story?

Paul: Oh, yeah. I meant to say *horse*.

Teacher: That makes more sense. Lots of people make mistakes like this one. Can you tell why people might make a mistake like this?

Paul: Probably because I only looked at the letters; I didn't think about whether it made sense or not.

Teacher: The letters in the words "house" and "horse" are very similar (demonstrates on the board). There are only two letters that are different. Sounding out words is a good strategy to use, but you need to ask yourself if the words make sense in the sentence or the story.

Dialogue 2:

Elyshia: I'm confused by this question that says, "Why do you think the character in the book you just read chose to take the action he or she took? What other actions could he or she have taken?" I don't know how to answer that. He did what he did. The author made up the story, so the author made him do it. What other answer is there?

Teacher: This question asks for your opinion. Maybe you could think about what you would have done if you had a choice to make.

MAKE SOME NOTES OF YOUR OWN BEFORE TURNING THE PAGE

Strengths:

Needs:

Strategies:

Response Ideas

Strengths:
- consistent use of graphophonemic cue system
- good sight vocabulary
- good oral language and vocabulary
- parent involvement

Needs:
- direct instruction for comprehension at all levels — literal, inferential, and critical thinking
- direct instruction for monitoring comprehension during reading
- use of various methods for monitoring student progress

Strategies:
- "Before" or "Into" reading strategies — activate background knowledge, make predictions, direct instruction in questioning techniques
- "During" or "Through" reading strategies — model answers to questions, especially inferential and open-ended; direct instruction for finding support in text; use journals to ask questions; make comments and jot down vocabulary while reading; use semantic and syntactic cues for monitoring comprehension; and use story frames (Cudd & Roberts, 1987; Fowler, 1982) or story grammars (Mandler & Johnson, 1977; Thorndyke, 1977), and other graphic organizers
- "After" or "Beyond" reading strategies — generate story frames and other graphic organizers, using a variety of genres; model reading by using think-alouds (Nist & Kirby, 1986; Randall, Fairbanks & Kennedy, 1986); ask high-level or open-ended questions to stimulate "grand conversations" (Peterson & Eeds, 1990) and increase interaction with the text; create readers theatre, puppet shows, art projects, and book response journals
- to monitor progress, choose materials that are appropriate to student reading level; base reading level on observations, reading analyses, running records, (Clay, 1979) or miscues with retelling (Goodman & Burke, 1970), student input via interest inventories and conferences
- for continued parent involvement, send home book bags, encourage retellings to parents, and conduct parent education seminars regarding building comprehension

Narrative:

This class needs direct instruction for comprehension at all levels — literal, inferential and critical thinking — and monitoring of comprehension during reading. The following strategies should be taught before, during and after reading: *Before* — activate background knowledge; make predictions. *During* — direct instruction in questioning techniques; model answers to questions on all levels; find support in text; have students ask questions, make comments, and jot down vocabulary while reading. *After* — use semantic and syntactic cues for monitoring comprehension; generate story frames and other graphic organizers using a variety of genres; model reading by using think-alouds; ask open-ended questions to stimulate "grand conversations" and increase interaction with the text; have students produce related art and drama projects and book response journals. To foster independence use silent sustained reading (SSR). In order to monitor progress, choose materials that are appropriate to student reading level; base levels on observations, reading analyses with retelling, and student input via interest inventories and conferences. For continued parent involvement, send home book bags, encourage retellings to parents, and provide parent education regarding building comprehension strategies.

DOMAIN III

8th Grade Group

"I have just talked to the parents at back-to-school night. I teach a core which includes English and Social Studies. A group of parents voiced their concerns that their children could read the words in their textbooks, but they didn't understand what they were reading. They said the kids had a hard time with homework that involved answering questions from their textbooks or looking up information in reference books. Further, they said that their kids don't do their homework without lots of prodding; the parents say it's a battle every night. The kids say homework is boring. I'm seeing the same thing. These six eighth graders (four boys, two girls) are giving me gray hair. They have excellent word attack skills and can read fluently, but they have trouble with main ideas, analyzing text, and taking notes in their learning logs (Atwell, 1990). How will I know what skills this group needs, and what instruction I should use? In addition to grades, how should I monitor their progress?"

MAKE SOME NOTES OF YOUR OWN BEFORE TURNING THE PAGE

Strengths:

Needs:

Strategies:

Rationale:

Response Ideas

Strengths:
- ability to decode text
- interested parents

Needs:
- strategies for comprehending expository text
- reference skills and study skills
- test taking skills
- inner motivation for doing homework
- increased self-esteem from some success around reading
- ability to differentiate purposes for reading different materials

Strategies:
- Prereading strategies — use KWL (Know, Want to Know, Learned) (Ogle, 1992), SQ3R (Survey, Question, Read, Recite, Review) (Robinson, 1941) or similar techniques to:
  —activate background knowledge of subject matter
  —preview text and vocabulary
  —make predictions
  —ask questions
  —set purposes for reading
  —adjust rate to material, such as reading carefully, skimming, and scanning
  —use learning logs and graphic organizers to record any of the prereading strategies above
- Study skills strategies — teacher should give direct instruction and model
  —structure of text (location of and criteria for main idea, patterns in paragraphs, such as simple list, time-order, compare/contrast, cause/effect, problem/solution, signal words, headings and subheadings, visuals, charts, graphs)
  —report writing (use of reference materials, vocabulary and idea cards, outlining, note taking)
  —memory strategies
  —test taking methods
  —using learning logs and graphic organizers to record and organize new learning

- ◆ "After" or "Beyond" strategies — teacher should give direct instruction and model
  —using learning logs and graphic organizers to summarize and reflect on learning
  —using performance assessments, such as problem-solving projects
- ◆ Vary homework assignments in type and length and allow students some choice in homework responses (some may choose to make a graphic organizer, others may want to respond in a paragraph, etc.)

Rationale:

- ◆ Giving specific strategies for each aspect of studying text allows students to have more control over their own learning
- ◆ Direct instruction and modeling of strategies allows students to learn the processes for studying which they can take with them and use throughout their school careers and beyond
- ◆ Allowing variations in responses to homework assignments may lessen resistance to homework

Narrative:

The students in this group need strategies for expository text, including pre-reading strategies, such as KWL or SQ3R (in order to activate background knowledge of subject matter; to preview text and vocabulary; make predictions, and ask questions; to set purposes for reading; and to adjust rate to material). They need to use learning logs and graphic organizers to record background knowledge, as well as to record, organize, reflect on and summarize new learning for assessment purposes. They need direct instruction and modeling of reference and study skills, such as structure of text (location of and criteria for main idea, and patterns in paragraphs, such as simple list, time-order, compare/contrast, cause/effect, problem/solution, signal words, headings and subheadings, etc.); report writing (use of reference materials, vocabulary and idea cards, outlining, note taking), memory strategies and test taking methods. There should be some variation in types and length of homework to allow students some choice and lessen resistance. Direct instruction and modeling of strategies gives students more control over their own learning.

DOMAIN III

6th Grade Class

In this sixth grade class of thirty-two students, comprised mostly
of English speakers at various levels of abilities and skills, the
teacher needs to devise some strategies to deal with some issues in
comprehension of literature. Most do not have a lot of difficulty
with word attack, but their reading comprehension scores on a
standardized test range from the 22nd percentile to the 65th percentile. The class engages in lively discussions around readings,
but because they don't always understand the story, they have a
hard time supporting their answers from the text. Given this information along with the following summaries (based on John
Steinbeck's The Pearl), describe what strategies you would use
and why.

Teacher Summary

The story takes place in a poor village in the tropics where Kino, the main character,
lives with his wife and baby. In this first chapter, the baby is bitten by a scorpion, but
because he thinks the family cannot pay, the doctor at first refuses to come to help.
Little does he know that Kino has just found a valuable pearl on a diving expedition.

Summary 1
Keenan lives in a small town. He got a bug bite and brought out the pearls.

Book Summary

Keenan lives in a small town. He got a bug bite and brought out pearls.

Summary 2
There were some poor people that lived in a village. One day there baby was stung by a scorpean every one came to look. the mother tryed to suck out the poisen but it didn't work that well so she said get the doctor but everyone knew the doctor would not come to them the doctor would only help the rich people so everyone in the village followed the mother and father to the doctors. He asked them if the had any money she pulled out a paper folder many times filled with 7 purals the doctor regected the 7 almost wourther (worthless) purals and said he had more immportant things to attend to.

There were some poor people that lived in a village. One day there baby was stung by a scoupeaine every one came to look the mother tryed to such out the poisen but it didn't work that well so she said get the doctor but everyone knew the doctor would not come to them the doctor would only help the rith people se everyone it the village followed the mother and father to the doctors. the asked them if the had any money she pulled and a paper folder many times filled with 7 purals the doutor regected the 7 almost wourther purals and said he had more immporton.g thing to attend to.

Summary 3

Their was this boy who had filings (feelings) bad and good and bad people were in it. It was like a dream. The boys name is Kinow. The dream was about this person who came and they were trying to do something to Kinow but Kinow wouldent let it happen.

Summary 4

The story sounds like Keno and his family are on a island. Keno is nature of the land or something like that. Keno is like a semarton (Samaritan) he always puts others needes infront of him self. When He was out side a scorpean came and stung the baby and the baby has a chance to die because of the poison. Keno and others knew about the scorpin and didn't anything about it. If they did this would have never happened.

MAKE SOME NOTES OF YOUR OWN BEFORE TURNING THE PAGE

Strengths:

Needs:

Strategies & Rationale:

Response Ideas

Strengths:
- word attack and word recognition skills
- oral language — ability to take an active part in oral discussions

Needs:
- to be able to self-monitor (Brown, 1980) (determine when reading is not making sense)
- to be able to synthesize and summarize main points of what has been read and/or discussed
- to be able to support ideas with references to specific parts of text

Strategies & Rationale:

- before reading, use think-aloud (Nist & Kirby, 1986; Randall, Fairbanks & Kennedy, 1986) strategy to show students how good readers monitor their own reading
  - read part of chapter or story aloud
  - make predictions as you read; confirm or correct your predictions
  - reread when text doesn't make sense
  - note parts that show major element of story — characters, plot, setting, major action (on board, overhead, or chart paper)
  - ask questions of yourself about parts of the text
  - point out parts of the text that support your understanding
- during reading, have students make predictions and take notes in their learning log or mark the places in the story or chapter where the reading does not make sense to them; doing this begins to get students in the habit of monitoring while they read
- after discussion,
  - discuss and practice using criteria for a main idea (not too broad, not a detail, not outside the topic); have students practice giving titles to short paragraphs
  - guide students in the use of graphic organizers (in the form of Venn diagrams, webs, or clusters), outlines, or notes to help students identify main points
- provide direct instruction and model writing summaries from graphic organizers so that students have a better understanding of the process of summary writing as well as what a summary actually looks like

Narrative:

Before reading, use the think-aloud strategy to show students how good readers monitor their own reading: make predictions as you read; confirm or correct your predictions; reread when text doesn't make sense; note parts that show major elements of story (characters, plot, setting, major action); ask questions; and point out parts of the text that support your understanding.

When students read have them make predictions, take notes in their learning logs, or mark the places in the story or chapter where the reading does not make sense to them. Doing this begins to get students in the habit of monitoring while they read. Discuss ideas and how they supported them. After discussion, practice using criteria for a main idea and guide students in the use of graphic organizers to identify main points. Model writing summaries from graphic organizers so that students have a better understanding of the process of summary writing as well as what a summary actually looks like.

Multiple Choice - Domain III

Question 1:

Mrs. Lemon does a read-aloud/think-aloud several times a week in her first grade classroom. What strategy is she not modeling:
- a) phonetic analysis
- b) making connections with the text
- c) asking questions of the text, author, and self
- d) checking predictions

Question 2:

Juan, Samir, Suzie, and Pat in Mr. Edward's fourth grade have difficulty with summarizing what they've read. Which would not be an effective strategy to address this problem:
- a) using a graphic organizer
- b) using reciprocal teaching
- c) modeling the summarizing process
- d) using the cloze procedure

Question 3:

Mr. Edwards also has several students in his fourth grade class that need more strategies for comprehension of text. Which of the following not is an effective strategy for a student to use:
- a) looking up vocabulary words during reading
- b) activating prior knowledge before reading
- c) using context clues for monitoring
- d) checking and modifying predictions while reading

Question 4:

Sets of instructional strategies that Mr. Edwards could use for improving comprehension that are similar to one another are:
- a) KWL and buddy reading
- b) QAR and SQ3R
- c) Graphic organizers and think-alouds
- d) Reciprocal teaching and Literature Circles

Question 5:

Ms. Redcloud gave an assessment of literary elements to her sixth grade class. Which of the following would be included on her list of elements:
   a)   setting and time
   b)   character
   c)   theme or moral
   d)   all of the above

Question 6:

In her book discussions Ms. Redcloud uses various levels of comprehension questions. First, she introduces the different types of questions. Next she models different types of questions using fairy tales. Finally, the students make up their own questions in the different categories. Ms. Redcloud's student Jose gave this question for discussion: "Why do you think Cinderella stayed in a situation where she was mistreated?" This is an example what type of question:
   a)   inference
   b)   literal
   c)   main event
   d)   critical thinking

Question 7:

Mrs. Malula has an eighth grade social studies class. They need note taking, outlining, and study skills. Which strategy should she begin to model, teach, and have students practice first:
   a)   patterns of expository text
   b)   reciprocal teaching
   c)   sequencing
   d)   main idea

Question 8:

Mr. Lutz recognizes the importance of supporting at-home reading for his third graders. Which of the following would not promote this program:

   a)   at back-to-school night model reading strategies for parents to use with their children
   b)   send book bags home as part of regular homework
   c)   have parental partnership to "Turn off the TV!"
   d)   use the Author's Chair

Answers to Domain III

Question 1:

a) phonetic analysis. Mrs. Lemon is not modeling phonetic analysis because she is an expert reader and has achieved fluency and thus automaticity in terms of phonetic analysis. During read-alouds/think-alouds Mrs. Lemon is demonstrating how an expert reader interacts with text during reading. Answers b), c) and d) are all examples of how a good reader interacts with text.

Question 2:

d) cloze procedure. Cloze procedure is an instructional tool for teaching students how to use context clues. Items a), b) and d) are effective strategies for teaching students who are having difficulty with summarizing; graphic organizers could be part of modeling the process of summarizing and reciprocal teaching provides good practice for summarizing.

Question 3:

a) looking up vocabulary words during reading is too time consuming and will interrupt the meaning-making process as a whole. Teaching the student to use context clues contributes to the meaning-making process and is more efficient and effective. Answers b) and d) allow readers to get ready to read the text, interact with the text, and monitor what they are reading.

Question 4:

d) reciprocal teaching and Literature Circles are similar. In each one, small groups of students assume the role of the teacher and discuss the text in-depth by asking questions, summarizing, making predictions, and clarifying the text. Answer a) KWL and buddy reading are not alike because the first deals with activating background knowledge, and adding to that knowledge and the second involves reading with a partner. Answer b) Questioning the Author and SQ3R are not similar because the first is a form of questioning and the second is a study strategy. Answer c) graphic organizers and think-alouds are not alike because one is a technique for visually organizing ideas, and the other is a method of modeling what good readers do.

Question 5:

d) Items a), b) and c) are all literary elements and each should be part of the instruction and discussion of good literature.

Question 6:

d) Jose's question requires critical thinking. Critical thinking questions require the reader to evaluate and use background knowledge to answer. Answer a) inference would involve putting together clues embedded in the story along with your background knowledge. Answer b) literal would be directly stated in the story. Answer c) main event would require the reader to chose the event that was most important to the story.

Question 7:

d) main idea. Mrs. Makula needs to teach her students how to locate the main idea first. Being able to determine the main idea is the basic component of note taking, outlining, and being able to study effectively. Answer a) patterns of expository text is important after students can tell the difference between relevant and irrelevant information in text. Answer b) reciprocal teaching is an instructional tool to facilitate students' interactions with the text. Answer c) graphic organizers would be useful in understanding expository text, but students still need to be able to identify main ideas before they can organize the information visually.

Question 8:

d) the Author's Chair. The Author's Chair is a component of Writer's Workshop. During this time the students share their writing with the class. Answers a), b), and c) all promote student reading.

DOMAIN IV

2nd Grade Class

This second grade class in a suburban setting has twenty students. The students are at various stages of literacy, from the emergent to the independent stage. At this point, the teacher would like to help them better understand how reading and writing are connected, and enable them to move beyond reading word-by-word. What techniques, methods, or strategies would you suggest?

MAKE SOME NOTES OF YOUR OWN BEFORE TURNING THE PAGE

Strengths:

Needs:

Strategies:

Response Ideas

Strengths:
- basic understanding of text
- some knowledge of skills

Needs:
- fluency and expression
- increase understanding of syntax and grammatical structure
- increase student ability to make connections between oral or spoken language and written text structures

Strategies:

- to increase fluency use choral reading which will allow students to
  —practice reading in phrases rather than word-by-word
  —recognize the role of punctuation in aiding expression and enhancing meaning
- use repeated readings of familiar texts
- use buddy reading or partner reading to practice in a smaller setting
- encourage students to use the tape recorder which will allow them to listen to their own reading
- to increase students' understanding of syntax and grammatical structure, while also increasing their ability to make connections between oral or spoken language and written text structures
  —use Readers Theatre (in which students rewrite a book or a story in play form)
  —have students present the finished product to an audience which will enhance reading fluency and oral language.

Narrative:
To increase fluency, use choral reading to practice phrase reading and teach the use of punctuation for expression and meaning. Use repeated readings of familiar texts, buddy reading or partner reading and tape recorders. Use Readers Theatre for a better understanding of syntax, grammatical structure, and oral connection to written language. Have students present the play to enhance oral language and fluency.

DOMAIN IV

7th Grade Class

This inner city seventh grade class has thirty-five students many of whom are second generation Hispanics. Although they generally have decoding skills and can understand the main points of the stories they read, they have difficulty with some other aspects of the text. Read the following excerpt from a class discussion on the book <u>Bridge to Teribithia</u> by Katherine Patterson and determine what strategies they need and why.

Discussion One

Teacher: Why was Jess reluctant to go to Teribithia without Leslie?

Students: (no immediate response)

Teacher: What do you think *reluctant* means?

Student One: Felt funny about it?

Teacher: Tell me more about that.

Student One: I'm not sure. I really didn't understand that.

Teacher: Do you think he wanted to go to Teribithia by himself?

Student Two: No.

Teacher: What makes you think so? Go back and read those lines at the bottom of page 65 and see if you can tell what it means by using the author's words.

(Students read.)

Student Three: I don't understand the magic thing.

Discussion Two

Teacher: What words did you write down in your journal that gave you trouble, that you didn't know?

Student One: I didn't know what *suppress* means.

Teacher: So, what strategy could you use when you run into a word you don't know?

Student One: Look it up in the dictionary.

Teacher: How else could you find out what it means.

Student One: Ask the teacher.

Teacher: We'll have to work on some other ways. Does anyone else have another word they wrote down?

Student Two: What does *a-b-s-o-r-b-e-d* mean? How do you say it?

Teacher: (Pronounces *absorbed*.) Do you remember that we had that word in science when we talked about how the roots of the plant *absorbed* all the water in the glass?

Student Three: But May Belle wasn't drinking any water. She was watching TV.

MAKE SOME NOTES OF YOUR OWN BEFORE TURNING THE PAGE

Strengths:

Needs:

Strategies:

Response Ideas

Strengths:

- ◆ can decode many words when reading
- ◆ can get the main points and events from text

Needs:

- ◆ work with decoding more difficult words
- ◆ work with vocabulary development
- ◆ increased knowledge of English syntax and grammatical structure

Strategies & Rationale:

- ◆ direct instruction and modeling the use of context and syntactical clues so that students don't have to stop and look up words
- ◆ direct instruction within the context of narrative and expository text combining the decoding of more difficult words with vocabulary and word study, such as
  —syllabication
  —word analysis (word origins, roots, suffixes, prefixes) so that students can learn different ways to build vocabulary
- ◆ direct instruction of multiple meanings within the context of narrative and expository text
- ◆ direct instruction and practice in identifying different grammatical structures in English and understanding how they affect comprehension of the text

Narrative:

Using narrative and expository text, students require teacher instruction and modeling the use of context and syntactical clues in order not to interrupt their reading. They need word analysis (syllabication, word origins, roots, suffixes, prefixes), multiple meanings for different ways to build vocabulary, and practice in identifying different grammatical structures in English and understanding how these affect comprehension of the text.

DOMAIN IV

4th Grade Individual

Byron is a fourth grader who is known as a "cool dude" by his classmates. He is at the independent reading stage; however, Byron does not choose to do any independent reading. Reading is not "cool" according to Byron. How would you help him to be more engaged with good literature and reading in general?

MAKE SOME NOTES OF YOUR OWN BEFORE TURNING THE PAGE

Strengths:

Needs:

Strategies:

Response Ideas

Strengths:
- is able to read independently
- has social skills

Needs:
- more exposure to quality literature
- better connections to different literary genres
- motivation to read independently

Strategies:
- hold individual conference with student to determine his interests beyond the world of the classroom
- for independent reading, provide many diverse types of materials that span different genres, such as mysteries, fantasy, biographies and autobiographies, etc.
- do book talks to stimulate interest in particular books (briefly discuss a little bit of the characters, plot, and setting, and stop when something interesting is about to happen); have students also do book talks, which can often stimulate motivation to read the book
- read aloud to the class using thought-provoking literature that has personal connections to the age group and the interests of the class

Narrative:
Hold individual conference with student to determine his interests beyond the world of the classroom. Provide a wide selection of materials that span different genres, such as mysteries or biographies. Have teacher and students give book talks to stimulate interest in particular books. Read aloud to the class using literature that has personal connections to students.

Multiple Choice - Domain IV

Question 1:

Mrs. Kalua has a class of fifth graders, half of whom are second language learners. Which of the following is the most difficult for the English language learners:
- a)   oral language syntax
- b)   LEA
- c)   multiple meanings
- d)   idioms

Question 2:

In her daily instructional plans to support English language learners with scaffolding strategies, which of the following would she be most likely to use:
- a)   realia
- b)   graphic organizers
- c)   double entry journals
- d)   a and b

Question 3:

Mrs. Kalua also needs to make decisions about her instructional plan for vocabulary development. Which of the following would not directly contribute to vocabulary development:
- a)   cloze procedure
- b)   semantic mapping
- c)   read alouds
- d)   sight words

Question 4:

Mrs. Dempsey has a new second grade class half of whom are second language learners in different stages of English language development. Which of the following methods would be most effective in determining strengths and needs in oral language development:

    a)   journal writing samples
    b)   observations and developmental checklists
    c)   reading comprehension questions
    d)   San Diego Quick

Question 5:

Mrs. Dempsey also needs to assess her students' writing. Which of the following methods would be most effective in determining strengths and needs in written language development:

    a)   a spelling test
    b)   a standardized test
    c)   writing samples
    d)   workbook pages

Answers for Domain IV

Question 1:

d) idioms because they are culturally outside of the English language learner's experience. Also, idioms are difficult because even though the words may be simple, they do not convey their everyday dictionary meaning. Answer c) multiple meanings is a close second, but the context of the sentence can help with those, and one of the meanings is generally found in the dictionary. Development of English language syntax (grammatical structure) and language experience approach (LEA) are both *helpful* to English language learners.

Question 2:

d), a), and b) Realia (objects) create concrete connections to new words and add tactile and kinesthetic dimensions to learning. Graphic organizers provide support for students having difficulty with the comprehension of text by organizing the information pictorially. The answer c) double entry journals, while helpful for readers and writers of English, may not be helpful for the various stages of English language learning.

Question 3:

d) sight words. While very useful in allowing readers to gain fluency, sight words alone do not expand meaningful vocabulary. Oral language development through c) read-alouds, a) cloze procedure and b) semantic mapping all help to increase word understanding.

Question 4:

b) observations and developmental checklists where a teacher can monitor the different phases and elements of oral language development. Listening to a student speak in formal and informal situations, is the best way to evaluate English language development. The answer a) journal writing samples deals with written language, answer d) the San Diego Quick deals with knowledge of words read in isolation, and the answer c) reading comprehension questions also deals with reading.

Question 5:

c) writing samples. As it is true that students only become writers by writing, so it is true that teachers can only assess writing by analyzing actual samples. A spelling test a) deals with words in isolation; even if a student does well on a spelling test, it doesn't mean that the student will spell the words correctly when writing. The answer d) workbook pages is incorrect for the same reason. Answer b) a standardized test does not provide diagnostic information in order to inform teaching.

DOMAINS I-IV

DOMAINS I-IV

First Grader

Frank is a first grader who will not turn six until November. English is Frank's first language. He comes from a middle class family with two parents, who read to him on a regular basis. He does actively participate in class discussions, even though there are times when he will make an error in syntax with verb forms like "runned" for "run."

At independent reading time, Frank chooses picture books and pours over the pictures, but does not spend much time focusing on the words. If he does choose a book with more words, it is usually a book about sharks or dinosaurs. Given the following assessments and the information above, tell where Frank is in his literacy development and what instruction you would design for him and why.

Checklist for Observing Concepts about Print

NAME

Frank S.

Time at school	K										
Front of book	✓										
Print contains message	✓										
Where to start	✓										
Left to right	✓										
Return sweep	✓										
Word by word matching	✓										
First and last	✓										
Print is right way up	✓										
Left page before right	✓										
Full stop	—										
Question mark	✓										
Capital and lower case letter correspondence	✓										
Letters — Recognizes difference/ knows the term.	✓										
Words	✓										
First and last letters of words	✓										
Capital letters	✓										
Comments											

This page is copyright-free

Legend

✓	knows
0	does not know
—	does not know
0✓	corrected by student

Table 5.1 **Alphabet Recognition Test**   *Frank S.*

A ✓ S ✓ D ✓ F ✓ G ✓ H ✓ J ✓

K ✓ L ✓ P ✓ O ✓ I ✓ U ✓ Y ✓

T ✓ R ✓ E ✓ W ✓ Q ✓ Z (X sc ✓) X ✓

C ✓ V ✓ B ✓ N ✓ M ✓

a ✓ s ✓ ⓓ (b) f ✓ g ✓ h ✓ ⓙ (i)

k ✓ l (i sc) ✓ p ✓ o ✓ i ✓ u ✓ y ✓

t ✓ r ✓ e ✓ w ✓ q (P) z (X sc ✓) x ✓

c ✓ v ✓ b ✓ n ✓ m ✓ a ✓ y ✓

g ✓ q (P) t ✓ a ✓ g ✓ t ✓ q (P)

From Margaret Ann Richek, et al. *Reading Problems: Assessment and Teaching Strategies* (Third Edition). Needham, Massachusetts: Allyn and Bacon, 1996

Table 5.2 Assessing Phonological Awareness: Blending and Segmenting

Directions: I am going to say some words in a special code and I want you to figure out the real word. If I say s/-/a/-/t/, you say *sat*. If I say /p/-/i/-/g/, you say *pig*.

Teacher says:	Expected Response	Student's Response
/d/-/i/-/g/	dig	dig
/p/-/u/-/l/	pull	pull
/b/-/e/-/d/	bed	bed
/f/-/a/-/s/-/t/	fast	fast
/s/-/o/-/f/-/t/	soft	soft

Directions: Now we will change jobs. If I say *bat*, you say /b/-/a/-/t/. If I say *feet*, you say /f/-/eee/-/t/.

Teacher says:	Expected Response	Student's Response
can	/c/-/a/-/n/	c/a/n
tell	/t/-/e/-/l/	t/e/l/l
dust	/d/-/u/-/s/-/t/	d/u/s/t
sit	/s/-/i/-/t/	s/i/t
fog	/f/-/o/-/g/	f/o/g

NOTE: When a letter is enclosed in brackets (//), this indicates that you should say the letter *sound*.

Frank S.

Table 5.3 Assessing Letter–Sound Correspondences: Beginning Letter Sounds

Practice: What is the beginning sound of *mat*? (Student should say /m/.) What letter makes that sound? (Student should say "M." If not, model and practice another word.)

Word	Beginning Sound	Beginning Letter
fish	/f/	f
little	/l/	l
ride	/r/	r
want	/w/	u
happy	/h/	h

From Margaret Ann Richek, et al. *Reading Problems: Assessment and Teaching Strategies* (Third Edition). Needham, Massachusetts: Allyn and Bacon, 1996

The Box and the Fox

^{dk dk} ^{dk dk}
The <u>old</u> fox <u>saw a</u> box.

<u>He</u> said, "<u>What</u> is <u>this</u>?"

The box <u>said</u>, "I am a box."

The fox <u>said</u>, "<u>What</u> is a box?"

The box said, "A box is a box. <u>What are</u> you?"

The fox said, "I am a fox."

The box said, "<u>What</u> is a fox?"

The fox said, "A fox is a fox."

<u>So</u>, a box is a <u>box and</u> a fox is a fox.

Frank S. — very slow word-by-word, but read whole story with help.

___ = did not know

Graded Reading Passages Test: Form B—Narrative

201

Graded Reading Passages Test: Form B—Narrative

Frank S.
Listening

COMPREHENSION CHECK

A Snowy Day (1)

		Probed Recall	Free Recall

INTRODUCTION: Please read this story to find out what two children like to do.

A Snowy Day

Bill and Kim looked out the window. They were very happy. It was snowing. They wanted to go out to play.

Bill and Kim could not wait to build something with the snow. When they went outside, they made two large balls. They put one on top of the other. Then they made one small ball. They put it on the very top. Then Bill and Kim used some sticks and stones. Now they were done.

L 1. What were the names of the two children in the story?
_____ ✓
(Bill and Kim)

L 2. Why were Bill and Kim very happy?
_____ ✓
(They saw it was snowing.)

L 3. How many balls of snow did Bill and Kim make?
_____ ✓
(3)

L 4. Where did they put the small ball?
_____ ✓
(on the top)

I 5. What do you think Bill and Kim built with the white flakes?
_____ ✓
(a snowman)

C 6. Could this story have happened? What makes you think so?
_____ ✓
(Accept any logical response, such as "Because the events sound real.") *Yes, because people really do build snowmen.*

Accountable Miscues

Full Miscues: _____ × 1 = _____

Half Miscues: _____ × $\frac{1}{2}$ = _____

TOTAL _____

Total Comprehension Errors *0*
(L & I)

Retell
The boys wanted to play in the snow.
They were using sticks and stones
to make a snowman.

From Ezra L. Stieglitz. *The Stieglitz Informal Reading Inventory.* (Second Edition) Boston, Massachusetts: Allyn and Bacon 1997

IbI 200PR 20CR 2
ot to Ys. RUz.

FRank

I buy Super Soakers at Toys-R-US.

MAKE SOME NOTES OF YOUR OWN BEFORE TURNING THE PAGE

Strengths:

Needs:

Strategies and Rationale:

Response Ideas

Strengths:
- literacy development is age appropriate
- is read to by parents and teacher
- actively participates in class discussions
- phonemic awareness — can segment and blend whole words
- can identify most letters with their corresponding sounds
- sight word vocabulary in early stages
- can read short sentences using predictable text
- listening comprehension — is able to retell story in sequence
- stays on task during independent reading
- attempts invented spelling — uses beginning and ending consonants and some vowels
- can write a complete sentence
- has some idea of word spacing, capital letters and periods

Needs:
- development time
- some work with continuing problems around verb forms (syntax) in oral language
- some work with continuing problems with reversals in letter identification in reading and writing
- practice with initial consonant sounds as in w, h, c, k
- sight vocabulary
- fluency
- focus on words in independent reading
- spelling (encoding) medial sounds, particularly vowels
- increased pencil control (fine motor control)

Strategies & Rationale:
- vocabulary extension and modeling of verb forms through read-alouds and oral language (most children outgrow this with time)
- increase sight vocabulary through immersion in environmental print such as, word walls (Cunningham, 1995), reading the room, sight word games, practice reading words in poems and chants (choral reading), keeping word book or dictionary, reading predictable books in shared reading and independent reading, practice using kinesthetic/tactile techniques (tracing, sandpaper letters)

- for increased word attack skills (decoding), make or use commercial word games with onsets and rimes, rhyming words, word families, read decodable text, practice with sound blending, practice with counting syllables (clapping, snapping fingers)
- for increased comprehension:

  —Before Reading (Into): use pre-reading strategies such as activating background knowledge about subject, guiding student through a picture walk, having him make predictions using title and pictures, and pre-teaching new or difficult vocabulary

  —During Reading (Through): ask questions during shared reading to check understanding and to check predictions; use oral cloze (Taylor, 1953; Meeks & Morgan, 1978) to encourage use of context clues (syntactic and semantic cue system) along with graphophonemic cues to self-monitor or cross check for meaning (ask: Does that word make sense? Does it look like the word in the story?)

  —After Reading (Beyond): ask high level, open-ended questions to increase student's interaction with text and encourage more in-depth discussion; use extension activities such as readers theatre, simple semantic maps/webs, reading response journal, acting out the story, puppet theater, and drawings which show main events in beginning, middle, and end to promote awareness of sequence
- for fluency: use repeated readings with choral reading, echo reading, buddy reading, tape recording student's reading, and independent reading
- for writing: give opportunities to generate text every day using word walls (Cunningham, 1995), personal and commercial dictionaries, word stretching games to increase ability to distinguish medial and ending sounds, interactive (McKenzie, 1986) or shared writing, spelling program around word patterns (cvc etc.), oral spelling games using individual chalkboards, Making Words (Cunningham, 1995), etc.
- language experience stories (reading back the student's own dictated text)
- for writing between the lines, use modeling, interactive writing, practice on slates and paper (fine motor skills will improve with time)
- direct instruction in reversals in reading and writing to encourage self-monitoring

Narrative:

Frank just entered the emergent reader stage based on several pieces of evidence: he is able to retell details in sequence when read to (listening comprehension); he has an appropriate speaking vocabulary, he has developed phonemic awareness; he is developing sight vocabulary; and he is starting to decode using initial consonants. He can write one sentence with invented spelling and has some concept of conventions of print.

Frank needs teacher read-alouds for extending his vocabulary and modeling how expert reading sounds. Frank can dictate language experience stories which promote fluency, sight vocabulary, decoding skills (graphophonemic cue system) and the application of semantic and syntactic cues systems. This strategy would be effective because the child is reading his own language, thus making the connection from speech to print. Frank also needs direct instruction in phonics, such as vowel sounds, onsets, and rimes (blends and word patterns), segmentation, rhymes, and syllables. These skills can be taught through activities such as letter and word games, individual slate work, centers, etc. Further, he needs to apply the decoding strategies by reading poems, chants, and predictable text that contain the phonics patterns previously taught.

Instruction in comprehension strategies should include the "Before" strategies of activating background knowledge, making predictions, picture walks and previewing new vocabulary. Instruction "During" reading should include shared reading to practice both phonics and comprehension strategies, oral cloze exercises to practice the use of context clues, and self-monitoring strategies (cross checking) for making meaning. In the "After" phase, to increase Frank's interaction with text, instruction should include practice in retelling, the use of critical thinking questions, in-depth discussion, semantic maps, drama, puppets, and drawings showing sequence of main events. In order to increase fluency and independence, Frank needs to reread familiar stories, using both choral reading and reading with a buddy.

In addition, Frank needs to generate text on a daily basis using word walls, word stretching, personal word books, as well as interactive writing.

Domains I-IV

Third Grader

Manuel is a third grader who speaks English but understands Tagalog and Spanish. At the beginning of the year as part of gaining baseline information, his teacher interviewed him, gave him an informal reading inventory and had him do a writing sample. During observations of his reading and writing behaviors in the first few days of school, the teacher noticed problems with fluency and confidence in reading. He was much more eager to do the writing sample than read. Given this information and the data below, chose one area of need in reading and one area of need in writing, and tell all the strategies the teacher could use to address these two needs.

Interview:

Teacher: Do you like to read?

Manuel: It depends on the book.

Teacher: What kinds of books do you like the best?

Manuel: I like books with lots of pictures because chapter books are harder.

Teacher: What do you do when you get stuck on a word when you're reading?

Manuel: I do the word by parts, cut them by places, like *to/day*.

Teacher: What do you do if that doesn't work?

Manuel: I go and ask somebody to tell me.

Teacher: What if no one is around?

Manuel: I sound it out.

Teacher: What do you think about writing?

Manuel: It's good, I like it.

Teacher: What do you like to write?

Manuel: I like to make really long stories like chapters.

Teacher: It appears that you like writing more than reading. Why is that?

Manuel: Cause I'm not saying the words, I'm writing the words how I think it is.

Scoring Sheet   3C (⊔)

Judy's class ~~was going on~~ a trip to visit an airport. *Before they* left *they* read

some books *about* airplanes *and* airplane pilots. *Everyone in* the class *was*

excited *when it came time to go.*

The class rode *to the* airport *in a* big yellow bus. *After the* bus stopped, *the*

first person *to get off was* Judy's teacher. *She* told the class that they must all stay

together *so that none of the students would get lost.*

First, *they* visited *the* ticket counter *and* learned how passengers buy their

tickets. *Then a* pilot came *and* told *them he would take them on a* large airplane.

After they were inside *the* airplane *everyone was* surprised *because it was so*

large. *When* Judy's class got back *to* school *they all said they* wanted *to* visit *the*

airport *again.*

Retell: *They went to a trip to the airport. They wanted to go to the airport again.*

Questions:

F 1. ___√___ Where was Judy's class going? (To visit an airport)
F 2. ___√___ What did they do before they left? (They read some books, or they read some books about airplanes and airplane pilots)
F 3. Don't know How did the class feel when it was time to go? (They were excited)
F 4. Don't know How did the class get to the airport? (They rode in a bus, or in a big yellow bus)
F 5. ___√___ Who was the first person to get off the bus? (Judy's teacher, or the teacher)
F 6. ___√___ What did the teacher tell the class when they first got off the bus? (That they must stay together, or that they must stay together so they would not get lost)
F 7. Don't know What did they visit first? (The ticket counter)
V 8. ___√___ In this story it said the students learned how the passengers buy their tickets. What is a passenger? (Someone who rides on an airplane)
F 9. ___X___ When the pilot came to meet the class what did he tell them? (He told them he would take them on an airplane, or on a large airplane)
I 10. Don't know What did the class say that would make you think they liked their visit to the airport? (They said they wanted to visit the airport again)

From Eldon E. Ekwall & James L. Shanker. *Ekwall/Shanker Reading Inventory.* (3rd Edition) Boston, MA: Allyn & Bacon, 1993

Succor

My Favoret thing to do is succor
I like being dyfens my taem is
the blue dyens

MAKE SOME NOTES OF YOUR OWN BEFORE TURNING THE PAGE

One Need in Reading:

One Need in Writing:

Strategies for Need in Reading:

Strategies for Need in Reading:

Response Ideas

Need in Reading: monitoring for meaning because he uses the graphophonemic cue system almost exclusively; most miscues result in loss of meaning

Strategies to Address Need in Reading:
- model use of semantic cue system through the use of context clues (reread, read on, go back and put in word that makes sense in the context)
- student practice with cloze procedure
- model the use of monitoring through read-alouds/think-alouds (self-correction of reading errors/miscues, ask questions about whether words make sense, ("*What is a pillot?*")
- student practice monitoring strategies
- within guided reading group, provide opportunity for pre-reading strategies (Into) such as pre-teaching vocabulary, activating background knowledge, scaffolding
- during (Through) reading provide scaffolding for student when he gets stuck on word or makes inappropriate substitutions
- after reading (Beyond) show student how monitoring will help him retell the story with greater detail and answer questions

Need in Writing: elaboration is the most serious concern since he is a third grader (mechanics are secondary)

Strategies to Address Need in Writing:
- teacher asks student to tell story orally, encourage detail by asking questions
- ask student to write about what he just said
- model elaboration in writing using overhead
- select examples of expert writers that show elaboration and detail
- have student evaluate two pieces of writing from a former class showing one with sparse details and one with more detail

Narrative:

Since Manuel uses graphophonemic cues almost exclusively, that many times result in a loss of meaning, he needs strategies for monitoring so that he brings meaning to text. Some of the strategies to teach this include modeling the use of the semantic cue system through the use of context clues, rereading, reading on, and going back to put in a word that makes sense in the sentence. He needs to add this strategy to his skills in grapho-phonemics. He can then practice with cloze procedure to use context. Another strategy the teacher can use is read-alouds/think-alouds to model monitoring, self-correcting and asking questions of himself about whether words make sense such as, "What is a pilot?" The student would then practice this procedure in a small group or with a partner. In addition, within his guided reading group, the teacher should provide opportunities for pre-reading strategies (Into stage) such as activating background knowledge, pre-teaching vocabulary and scaffolding with a picture walk and making predictions. The teacher can also teach monitoring strategies during reading (Through stage) by providing instruction when Manuel gets stuck on a word or makes inappropriate substitutions. After reading (Beyond stage) the teacher can show the student how monitoring will help the student retell the story with greater detail and answer the questions.

In writing, although Manuel needs support for spelling and other mechanics such as capitalization and punctuation, his major need is for elaboration in his pieces. While in the interview he says he prefers writing over reading, and he says he likes to make really long stories, he wrote very little for the writing sample. In order for Manuel to add detail to his writing, the teacher can ask him to tell the story orally, encouraging details by asking questions to clarify what he's saying. Then the teacher can ask him to write down what he just said. Another instructional strategy the teacher could use is to model elaboration in writing using her own text on the overhead. She could also show students examples of expert writers that demonstrate elaboration and detail. Additionally, she can have students compare and evaluate two pieces of writing from a former class showing one with sparse details and one with more detail.

Domains I-IV

Fourth Grader

Ramon is a first semester fourth grader. Tagalog is Ramon's first language; he moved to the United States the previous year. Although he is fairly proficient orally in English during informal class situations and outside with his peers, his shy demeanor prevents him from participating in class discussions. When asked to evaluate his reading, Ramon said he "just reads words" and forgets what he reads. He wants to read bigger vocabulary words so he can read Goosebumps books (chapter books). Writing samples show Ramon's problems in the area of grammatical structure for both words and sentences. His oral reading and retelling assessment is attached. His standardized achievement test scores from the prior year show:

- reading at 2.8 grade level (20th percentile)
- vocabulary skills at the 2.0 grade level (6th percentile)
- spelling skills at the 3.0 grade level (23rd percentile)
- English language usage skills at the 2.2 grade level (12th percentile)

What kinds of instructional strategies would you use for Ramon and why would you use these strategies?

Kamon

Graded Words in Isolation Test: Form A

229

Grade 2

		Flashed	Delayed
1.	low		
2.	deer		
3.	few		
4.	afraid		
5.	rest		
6.	mile		
7.	such		
8.	I'd		
9.	carry		
10.	puppy		
11.	owl		
12.	seven		
13.	quick		
14.	mountain		
15.	visit		
16.	follow		
17.	dragon		
18.	anyone		
19.	farmer		
20.	evening		
		_____ %	

Grade 3

		Flashed	Delayed
1.	crop	✓	
2.	force	✓	
3.	motor	✓	
4.	usual	✓	
5.	yesterday		✓
6.	bother		✓
7.	enjoy	✓	
8.	history	✓	
9.	nibble	✓	
10.	scratch	✓	
11.	parent	✓	
12.	television	✓	
13.	whisker		✓
14.	treat	✓	
15.	accident		✓
16.	dare	—	—
17.	understood		✓
18.	notebook		✓
19.	amaze	—	—
20.	familiar	—	—
		_85_ %	

From Ezra L. Stieglitz. *The Stieglitz Informal Reading Inventory.*
(Second Edition) Boston, Massachusetts: Allyn and Bacon 1997

Graded Reading Passages Test: Form D—Narrative

N The Blind Woman (3)

INTRODUCTION: Please read this story about a woman who could not see.

The Blind Woman

    A woman who had become blind called a doctor. She promised that if he could cure her, she would reward *reword* him well. If he failed, he would get nothing. The doctor agreed.

    He went often to the woman's apartment. He would pretend to treat her eyes. But he would also steal *faniter* furniture and other objects. Little by little, he took all her belongings. Finally, he used his skill to cure *Care* her and asked for his money.

    Every time he asked for his payment, the woman made up a reason for not paying him. Eventually he took her to court. The woman said to the judge, "I did promise to pay the doctor if he gave me back my sight. However, how can I be cured? *Cured dK* If I truly could see, wouldn't I see furniture *faniter* and other belongings in my house?"

L - Literal
I - Inferential

COMPREHENSION CHECK

		Probed Recall	Free Recall
L 1.	Who did the woman ask for help? (a doctor)	___	✓
L 2.	What promise did the woman make to the doctor? (to pay him well only if he cured her)	✓	___
L 3.	What did the doctor do while in the woman's apartment? (took furniture) (took all her belongings)	___	✓
L 4.	Why did the doctor take the woman to court? (because he wanted his payment)	___	✓
I 5.	Why didn't the woman want to pay the doctor for curing her blindness? (She felt he didn't deserve to be paid because he was a thief.)	✗	___
C 6.	What would you do if you were the judge in this case? (Accept any logical response, such as "I would place the doctor in jail for being dishonest.")	_✓_ _

Total Comprehension Errors   / I
(L & I)

Retell

A doctor promise a blind woman to make her see again. She promise to pay him. She not pay him because he took her stuff -- She say if she can see, where is her stuff?

From Ezra L. Stieglitz. *The Stieglitz Informal Reading Inventory*. (Second Edition) Boston, Massachusetts: Allyn and Bacon 1997

Quick Write

For I have 1 chah
to go araunn the ward
I go to philipnes becouse
I born in philipnes and my
Parent born in philipnes
and in philipnes is not very
cold and hot very hot
and in the philipnes more rain
drown in the ground, plants,
trees, and ocean and in philipnes
the peppole helping

Final Draft

for I have one chansh
to go around the world I will go to
philipnes because in the the air in the
the philipnes is not very cold and the
fruit is dirish and the trees
of philipnes are taller and in the morning the
sun is beoutiful and
the pbnts up and up and the rain
down in the ruit of the tree and
I hir at the bird singing in the trees
and the dogs are say raray, rara, and raw,

and I feeling in the philipnes
I happy and the grass flowus treeg
and ground are very bediful

and in the philipnes the rain is
beautiful see in the widows are in
dars and fruit of papay is good
in the philipns and

MAKE SOME NOTES OF YOUR OWN BEFORE TURNING THE PAGE

Strengths:

Needs:

Strategies and Rationale:

Response Ideas

Strengths:
- has some word recognition and decoding skills
- can communicate in English in day-to-day interactions (pragmatics)
- has self-knowledge about his strengths and weaknesses (metacognition)
- knows two languages
- has motivation to learn

Needs:
- comprehension strategies, monitoring
- increased word recognition skills, including the use of context
- increased vocabulary
- to understand that the purpose for reading is to read for meaning
- to know the traits that exemplify good readers
- confidence to participate in class discussions
- more control over written language — syntax (grammar)

Strategies and Rationale:
- Before reading (Into)
  - —needs pre-reading or scaffolding strategies such as activating background knowledge, supplying additional background knowledge needed to understand the story (first hand experiences or through discussion), previewing of new vocabulary, making predictions, writing new words in his own dictionary
  - —read-alouds to model English language structure, fluency and expression
- During reading (Through)
  - —needs guided reading using appropriate materials with regard to reading level and interest
  - —needs to read in small chunks (paragraphs or single pages)
  - —needs to reinforce vocabulary through use of context
  - —needs teacher modeling of monitoring (rereading, asking questions throughout text, checking predictions) for eventual self-monitoring
- After reading (Beyond)
  - —use graphic organizers to better understand main ideas and connections in the text
  - —have student make drawings depicting elements of literature (character, plot, setting, conflict, resolution)

—use dramatic plays as a tool to interpret story

—use structural analysis for vocabulary word building (prefixes, suffixes, root words, multiple meanings)

—use reading response journals to allow student to react to the text by making personal connections

- Have student take part in Literature Circles (Eeds & Wells, 1989; Peterson & Eeds, 1990; Samway et.al., 1994; Smith, 1990; Daniels, 1994) (small groups reading the same material; can be integrated with buddy or partner reading; discuss story in small group)

  —Literature Circles build confidence in discussion skills because students have an opportunity to rehearse discussion in small group setting which will then generalize to the larger group

- For writing, help student see connection between oral and written language

  —provide many examples of language

  —model writing in front of students, thinking out loud as the draft progresses

  —provide opportunities on a daily basis for student to write authentic pieces

  —teach the editing process

  —teach grammatical structures and conventions based on those that confuse Ramon — tenses, parallel structure, run-on sentences, use of capitals and punctuation

  —have student edit and proofread whole piece for just one structure or convention at a time

Narrative:

Ramon needs to have a better understanding of the reading process so that he can expect reading to have meaning for him. The teacher needs to discuss what good readers do and help Ramon apply these traits to his own reading. At the fifth grade level, students need to have both fluency and comprehension. Ramon has some word recognition and decoding skills, but he will need additional skills, including monitoring word endings, to have control over fluency. Ramon needs to be taught additional strategies for word identification and word attack, which include both phonics and structural analysis (prefixes, suffixes, root words) and a systematic vocabulary development program that includes the use of context clues. Since he has little meaning for many of the words that he identifies, he can preview the text before reading and write unknown words in a journal. Then the teacher can supply additional background knowledge needed to understand the story (first-hand experiences or through read-alouds). Furthermore, the teacher can model pre-reading strategies such as activating student background knowledge, making predictions, previewing new vocabulary and allowing time to practice these strategies and use them independently.

During reading, Ramon needs some guidance through the text to monitor comprehension in small chunks (paragraphs or single pages). He needs to check predictions, reinforce vocabulary and have teacher modeling of questioning for eventual self-monitoring.

After reading, he should use graphic organizers to better understand connections in the text and then react to the text in a reading response journal. Ramon should take part in Literature Circles because they allow discussion and rehearsal of ideas in a safe, small group setting. Such activities can enhance his comprehension skills, discussion skills and confidence.

To help Ramon make the connection between oral and written text, point out the similarities and, through the editing process, teach the grammatical structures that confuse Ramon, such as parallel structure and run-on sentences. Writing authentic pieces on a daily basis will help facilitate his progress in writing.

DOMAINS I-IV

Sixth Grader

Madeline is a sixth grader who has fair word attack skills but lacks fluency because she reads without expression and ignores punctuation. This interferes with her comprehension; she does not monitor what she reads. She is not able to retell a passage or answer questions on the various levels of understanding. Her scores on a standardized test as well as on an individualized reading assessment show that her word attack skills are on the fourth grade level and that her comprehension skills are on the third grade level. Madeline is an avid viewer of television learning stations. This gives her the opportunity to absorb much information about history and science. In her textbooks, she relies heavily on picture cues, graphs and charts and uses her background knowledge to fill in the gaps. Therefore, she gets good grades in subjects such as science and social studies. Because of her extensive background knowledge, she is able to actively participate in some class discussions, but her ideas are not always pertinent to the book under discussion. She has a rich vocabulary which is evident in her speech and writing (see sample below). However, she does not read books for enjoyment.

What would you recommend for instruction and how would you monitor her progress?

Madeline

The Human & keleton, has 206 Bones in the body
Ther joints help the bones move around.
Muscles give the bones flexibility.
There are about 602 muscles in the body.
The bones hold up the body by
providing structure.

MAKE SOME NOTES OF YOUR OWN BEFORE TURNING THE PAGE

Strengths:

Needs:

Strategies and Rationale:

Response Ideas

Strengths:
- uses background knowledge
- has some word attack skills
- has fair amount of knowledge of vocabulary
- participates in discussions
- uses visuals to comprehend textbooks
- relates well to content material
- absorbs information from other sources besides reading

Needs:
- to increase comprehension strategies
- to achieve fluency in reading
- to have more independent practice in reading
- to connect background knowledge and vocabulary to reading

Comprehension Strategies

For Narrative Text (story material)

Using a small group, whole class, or Literature Circles approach, model and coach the student to use the following:

Before Reading (Into):
- use background knowledge to make predictions about story using title
- have student select some key vocabulary to preview
- use vocabulary to confirm or correct previous prediction
- record students predictions on board, on chart paper, or in student journal
- help students make a graphic organizer (semantic map, visual representation of ideas), using background knowledge to brainstorm ideas about setting (for instance, Diary of Anne Frank: knowledge of the Holocaust and World War II)

Durring Reading (Through):

- do think-alouds (Nist & Kirby, 1986; Randall, Fairbanks & Kennedy, 1986) (model how text sounds and how good readers construct meaning as they read)
- set purpose for reading — to check prediction
- break down passage into manageable chunks
- to teach monitoring of comprehension, using reading response journals have student note ideas, questions, and parts of the text that are confusing (add page numbers)
- use reciprocal teaching (have students generate questions, clarify answers or ideas with partner, retell, or summarize sequence of events to partner or group)
- reread to apply fix-up strategies when confused

After Reading (Beyond):

- use graphic organizers (semantic webs) to detail elements of literature (setting, characters, theme, conflict, etc.)
- use questions to stimulate discussions that require literal, inferential, analytical, evaluative, and connective thinking (personal connections to story)
- show student how to look back into text to support answers
- have student write reactions and responses in journals
- have student write descriptions in the style of the author or genre

Building Fluency and Independent Reading:

- do book talks with student to stimulate interest in fiction
- do creative dramatics to encourage fluency and expression
- do teacher read-alouds to model fluency and expression (phrase reading in particular)
- provide many and different types of materials and genres from which students can choose
- give alternative assignments to book reports to accommodate different learning styles

Comprehension Strategies

For Expository Material (factual text)

Using a small group or whole class, model and coach student to use the following:

- use the content area textbook and other reference material for locating and retrieving and information, such as:
  —predicting
  —previewing
  —activating background knowledge
  —organization of text (location of main idea in paragraphs, signal words, patterns in paragraphs)
- use the content area textbook and other reference material for retaining information using such strategies as:
  —note taking
  —outlining
  —summarizing
  —graphic organizers
  —report writing
- strategies above reflect techniques contained in SQ3R (Study, Question, Read, Recite, Review) (Robinson, 1941) and KWL (Know, Want to Know, Learn) (Ogle, 1992)

Ongoing Assessment:

- use periodic conferences and informal reading inventories (add retelling immediately following oral reading), and ask questions on various levels (literal, inferential, and critical thinking), to check on comprehension and monitoring
- use teacher-made tests such as cloze procedure, essays, performance assessments
- analyze standardized testing to determine whether student is able to show what she knows on measures which are timed and require silent reading

Narrative:

Because of the word attack skills she has in place, Madeline does not struggle over every word. However, she does not really have fluency, and therefore, she has little comprehension. For narrative text, Madeline needs to use strategies before reading such as activating background knowledge with semantic maps (graphic organizers) and previewing and making predictions. During reading, she needs modeling of think-alouds.

She needs to read to check predictions, break down passages into smaller sections and to monitor comprehension by noting ideas in a reading response log as she goes along. She needs to be involved in reciprocal teaching to generate questions, clarify answers, summarize with a partner, and to apply fix-up strategies when reading doesn't make sense. After reading, she needs to use semantic webs to detail elements of literature. She should answer questions that require literal, inferential, analytical, evaluative, and connective thinking. She should locate support for her answers in the text, and write responses in her journal.

For expository text, Madeline needs modeling of strategies for textbooks and reference material such as predicting, previewing vocabulary and concepts, activating background knowledge (SQ3R or KWL), determining organization of text (location of main idea, signal words, patterns like comparison-contrast, cause-effect), note taking, outlining, summarizing, using graphic organizers, and report writing.

In order to build reading fluency and independent reading, Madeline needs to hear book talks and participate in Literature Circles, be involved in creative dramatics and listen to teacher read-alouds. The teacher might also assign alternative forms of book reports to stimulate her interest in reading.

The teacher should periodically assess Madeline's progress by recording her oral readings and retellings and cloze procedure to check comprehension and monitoring strategies. She also needs to learn self-assessment through developing a portfolio which includes the tapes of her reading and shows her growth over time. Standardized tests can be used to determine progress in silent, timed reading.

REFERENCES

Adams, Marilyn. (1990) *Beginning to Read: Thinking and Learning About Print.* Cambridge, Massachusetts: MIT Press.

Adams, Marilyn, Barbara R. Foorman, Ingvar Lundberg, & Terri Beeler. (1998) *Phonemic Awareness in Young Children.* Baltimore, Maryland: Paul H. Brookes Publishing Co.

Atwell, Nancie. (1986) *In the Middle: Writing, Reading and Learning with Adolescents.* Portsmouth, New Hampshire: Boynton/Cook.

Bear, Donald, Invernizzi, Marcia, Templeton, Shane and Johnston, Francine. (1995) *Words Their Way: Word Study for Phonics, Vocabulary, and Spelling.* Englewood Cliffs, New Jersey: Prentice-Hall.

Blatt, Gloria, T. Ed. (1993) *Once Upon a Folk Tale: Capturing the Folklore Process with Children.* New York, New York: Teachers College Press.

Bosma, Bette. (1992) *Fairy Tales, Fables, Legends, and Myths: Using Folk Literature in Your Classroom.* New York, New York: Teachers College Press.

Brown, H. & Cambourne, Brian. (1987) *Read and Retell.* Portsmouth, New Hampshire: Heinemann.

California State Board of Education and California Commission for the Establishment of Academic Content and Performance Standards. *Language Arts: Reading, Writing Listening, and Speaking: Content Standards for Grades K-12.* Sacramento, California: California Department of Education.

Carnine, D. W., Silbert, J. & Kameenue, E. J. (1997) *Direct Instruction Reading* (Third edition). Englewood Cliffs, New Jersey: Prentice-Hall, Inc.

Clay, Marie. (1991) *Becoming Literate.* Portsmouth, New Hampshire: Heinemann.

Cunningham, P. M. (1995) *Phonics They Use: Words for Reading and Writing* (Second Edition). New York: HarperCollins.

Daniels, H. (1994). *Literature Circles: Voice and Choice in the Student-Centered Classroom.* York, Maine: Stenhouse Publishers

Davies Samway, K. & Whang, G. (1996) *Literature Study Circles in a Multicultural Classroom.* York, Maine: Stenhouse Publishers.

Farr, Roger & Tone, B. (199) *Portfolios and Performance Assessment.* Orlando, Florida: Harcourt Brace.

*Fountas, I. C. & Pinnell, G. S. (1996) *Guided Reading: Good First Teaching for All Children.* Portsmouth, New Hampshire: Heinemann.

Graves, M. F., Juel, C. & Graves, B.B. (1998) *Teaching Reading in the 21st Century.* Needham Heights, Massachusetts: Allyn & Bacon.

Graves, Donald H. (1994) *A Fresh Look At Writing.* Portsmouth, New Hampshire: Heinemann.

Gunning, T. G. (1998) *Assessing and Correcting Reading and Writing Difficulties.* Needham Heights, Massachusetts: Allyn & Bacon.

*Gunning, T. G. (1996) *Creating Reading Instruction for All Children* (Second Edition). Needham Heights, Massachusetts: Allyn & Bacon.

Irwin, Judith Westphal. (1990) *Teaching Reading Comprehension Processes* (Second Edition). Englewood Cliffs, New Jersey: Prentice-Hall.

Henderson, Edmund H. & James Bears. (1980) *Developmental and Cognitive Aspects of Learning to Spell.* Newark, Delaware: International Reading Association.

Holdaway, D. (1979) *The Foundations of Literacy.* New York: Ashton Scholastic.

Lapp, Diane, James Flood, & Nancy Farnan (Eds.) (1996) *Content Area Reading and A Learning: Instructional Strategies* (Second Edition) Needham Heights, Massachusetts: Allyn & Bacon.

Lynch, P. (1986) *Using Big Books and Predictable Books.* Richmond Hill, Ontario: Scholastic-TAB.

Peregoy, S. & Boyle, O. (1997) *Reading, Writing, and Learning in ESL: A Resource Book for K-12 Teachers*. White Plains, New York: Longman.

Peterson, Ralph & Eeds, Maryann. (1990) Grand Conversations: Literature Groups in Action. Ontario, Canada: Scholastic Canada Ltd.

*Reutzel, D. R. & Cooter, Jr., R. B. (1996) *Teaching Children to Read: From Basals to Books*, Second Edition. Englewood Cliffs, New Jersey: Prentice-Hall, Inc.

Richek, M. A., Schudt Caldwell, J., Holt Jennings, J. & Lerner, J.W. (1996) *Reading Problems: Assessment and Teaching Strategies*. Needham Heights, Massachusetts: Allyn & Bacon.

*Ruddell, R. B. & Rapp Ruddell, M. (1995). *Teaching Children to Read and Write*. Needham Heights, Massachusetts: Allyn & Bacon.

*Ruddell, R. B. (1999) *Teaching Children to Read and Write* (Second edition). Needham Heights, Massachusetts: Allyn & Bacon.

*Sampson, M., Sampson, M. B. & Van Allen, R. (1995) *Pathways to Literacy*. Fort Worth, Texas: Harcourt Brace College Publishers.

Schipper, B. & Rossi, J. (1997). *Portfolios in the Classroom*. York, Maine: Stenhouse Publishers.

Strickland, Dorothy S. (1998) *Teaching Phonics Today: A Primer for Educators*. Newark, DE: International Reading Association.

*Tompkins, G.E. (1997). *Literacy for the 21st Century*. Englewood Cliffs, New Jersey: Prentice-Hall, Inc.

Tompkins, G. E. & Hoskisson, K. (1995) *Language Arts: Content and Teaching Strategies*. Englewood Cliffs, New Jersey: Prentice-Hall, Inc.

Vacca, Richard T. & Joanne L Vacca. (1993) *Content Area Reading* (Fourth Edition) New York: HarperCollins.

Yopp, Hallie Kay. "Developing Phonemic Awareness in Young children." *The Reading Teacher*, 45, 696-703, 1992.

Yopp, Ruth Helen & Yopp, Hallie Kay. (1992) *Literature-Based Reading Activities.* Needham Heights, Massachusetts: Allyn & Bacon.

The following texts are recommended for reference for their in-depth coverage of:

Phonics and Systematic Phonics Instruction
Phonemic Awareness —
Decodable Text & Predictable Text

Adams, Marilyn. (1990) *Beginning to Read: Thinking and Learning About Print.* Cambridge, Massachusetts: MIT Press.

Adams, Marilyn, Barbara, Foorman, Ingvar Lundberg, & Beeler, Terri. (1998) *Phonemic Awareness in Young Children.* Baltimore, Maryland: Paul H. Brookes Publishing Co.

Atwell, Nancie. (1986) *In the Middle: Writing, Reading and Learning with Adolescents.* Portsmouth, New Hampshire: Boynton/Cook.

Bear, Donald, Invernizzi, Marcia, Templeton, Shane, & Johnston, Francine. (1995) *Words Their Way: Word Study for Phonics, Vocabulary, and Spelling.* Englewood Cliffs, New Jersey: Prentice-Hall.

*Burns, Paul C., Roe, Betty D., & Ross, Elinor P. (1996) *Teaching Reading in Today's Elementary Schools.* Boston, Massachusetts: Houghton Mifflin Co.

Carnine, D. W., Silbert, J. & Kameenui, E. J. (1997) *Direct Instruction Reading* (Third Edition). Englewood Cliffs, New Jersey: Prentice-Hall, Inc.

Clay, Marie. (1991) *Becoming Literate.* Portsmouth, New Hampshire: Heinemann.

Cunningham, P. M. (1995) *Phonics They Use: Words for Reading and Writing* (Second Edition). New York: HarperCollins.

Fountas, I. C. & Pinnell, G. S. (1996) *Guided Reading: Good First Teaching for All Children.* Portsmouth, New Hampshire: Heinemann.

Gunning, T. G. (1998) *Assessing and Correcting Reading and Writing Difficulties.* Needham Heights, Massachusetts: Allyn & Bacon.

Strickland, Dorothy S. (1998) *Teaching Phonics Today: A Primer for Educators.* Newark, DE: International Reading Association.

Yopp, Hallie Kay. "Developing Phonemic Awareness in Young children." *The Reading Teacher*, 45, 696-703, 1992.

Comprehension and Comprehension Strategies:

Brown, A.L. (1980) Metacognitive Development and Reading. In R.J.Spiro, B.C. Bruce, & W.F. Brewer (Eds.). *Theoretical Issues in Reading Comprehension.* Hillsdale, New Jersey: Erlbaum.

Brown, H. & Cambourne, Brian. (1987) *Read and Retell.* Portsmouth, New Hampshire: Heinemann.

Clay, Marie. (1979) *The Early Detection of Reading Difficulties: A Diagnostic Survey with Recovery Procedures.* (Second Edition). Auckland, New Zealand: Heinemann.

Cudd, E.T. & Roberts, L.L. Using Story Frames to Develop Reading Comprehension in a First Grade Classroom. *The Reading Teacher*, 41 (1), 74-81. 1987.

Fowler, G.L. Developing Comprehension Skills in Primary Students Through the Use of Story Frames. *The Reading Teacher*, 36 (2), 176-179. 1982

Goodman, Yetta & Burke, C.L.(1970) *Reading Miscue Inventory Manual Procedure for Diagnosis and Evaluation.* New York: Macmillan.

Graves, M. F., Juel, C. & Graves, B.B. (1998) *Teaching Reading in the 21st Century.* Needham Heights, Massachusetts: Allyn & Bacon.

Gunning, T. G. (1998) *Assessing and Correcting Reading and Writing Difficulties.* Needham Heights, Massachusetts: Allyn & Bacon.

*Gunning, T. G. (1996) *Creating Reading Instruction for All Children* (Second Edition). Needham Heights, Massachusetts: Allyn & Bacon.

Irwin, Judith Westphal. (1990) *Teaching Reading Comprehension Processes* (Second Edition). Englewood Cliffs, New Jersey: Prentice-Hall.

Mandler, J. & Johnson, N. Remembrance of Things Parsed: Story Structure and Recall. *Cognitive Psychology,* 9, 111-151. 1977

Meeks, J.W. & Morgan, R.F. Classroom and the Cloze Procedure; Interaction in Imagery. *Reading Horizons*, 18, 261-264. 1978

Nist, S.L. & Kirby K. Teaching Comprehension and Study Strategies Through Modeling and Thinking Aloud. *Reading Research and Instruction*, 25, 254-264, 1986

Ogle, Donna (1992) KWL in Action: Secondary Teachers Find Applications that Work. In E.K. Dishner, T.W. Bean, J.E. Readence & D.W. Moore (Eds.) Content Area Reading: Improving Classroom Instruction. (Third Edition) Dubuque, Iowa: Kendall/Hunt.

Randall, A., Fairbanks, M.M., & Kennedy, M.L. Using Think-Aloud Protocols Diagnostically with College Readers. *Reading Research and Instruction*, 25, 240-253. 1986.

*Reutzel, D. R. & Cooter, Jr., R. B. (1996) *Teaching Children to Read: From Basals to Books*, (Second Edition). Englewood Cliffs, New Jersey: Prentice-Hall, Inc.

*Ruddell, R. B. & Rapp Ruddell, M. (1995). *Teaching Children to Read and Write.* Needham Heights, Massachusetts: Allyn & Bacon.

*Ruddell, R. B. (1999) *Teaching Children to Read and Write* (Second Edition). Needham Heights, Massachusetts: Allyn & Bacon

Taylor, W.L. Cloze Procedure: A New Tool for Measuring Readability. *Journalism Quarterly*, 30, 360-368, 1953.

Thorndyke, P. Cognitive Structures in Comprehension and Memory of Narrative Discourse. *Cognitive Psychology*, 9,97-110. 1977

Writing, Interactive Writing, Conferences, Writing Process

Atwell, Nancie. (1986) *In the Middle: Writing, Reading and Learning with Adolescents.* Portsmouth, New Hampshire: Boynton/Cook.

Graves, Donald H. (1994) *A Fresh Look At Writing*. Portsmouth, New Hampshire: Heinemann.

Gunning, T. G. (1998) *Assessing and Correcting Reading and Writing Difficulties.* Needham Heights, Massachusetts: Allyn & Bacon.

McKenzie, Moira. 1986. *Journeys Into Literacy.* Huddersfield, England: Schofield & Sims.

Tompkins, G. E. & Hoskisson, K. (1995) *Language Arts: Content and Teaching Strategies.* Englewood Cliffs, New Jersey: Prentice-Hall, Inc.

Assessment, Miscue Analysis, Running Records, Retellings, Portfolios, Cloze Procedure.

Brown, Hazel & Cambourne, Brian. (1987) *Read and Retell.* Portsmouth, New Hampshire: Heinemann.

Burns, Paul C. & Roe, Betty D. (1985) *Informal Reading Inventory: Preprimer to Twelfth Grade.* Boston, Massachusetts: Houghton Mifflin Company.

Ekwall, Eldon E. & Shanker, James L. (1993) *Ekwall/Shanker Reading Inventory (3rd Edition)* Needham Heights, Massachusetts: Allyn & Bacon

Farr, Roger & Tone, B. (199) *Portfolios and Performance Assessment.* Orlando, Florida: Harcourt Brace.

Clay, Marie M. (1993) *An Observation Survey of Early Literacy Achievement.* Portsmouth, New Hampshire: Heinemann.

*Fountas, I. C. & Pinnell, G. S. (1996) *Guided Reading: Good First Teaching for All Children.* Portsmouth, New Hampshire: Heinemann.

Gunning, T. G. (1998) *Assessing and Correcting Reading and Writing Difficulties.* Needham Heights, Massachusetts: Allyn & Bacon.

Richek, M. A., Schudt Caldwell, J., Holt Jennings, J. & Lerner, J.W. (1996) *Reading Problems: Assessment and Teaching Strategies.* Needham Heights, Massachusetts: Allyn & Bacon.

Schipper, B. & Rossi, J. (1997). *Portfolios in the Classroom.* York, Maine: Stenhouse Publishers.

Stieglitz, Ezra L. (1997). *The Stieglitz Informal Reading Inventory*. (Second Edition) Needham Heights, Massachusetts: Allyn & Bacon.

Sucher, Floyd & Allred, Ruel A. (1981) *The New Sucher-Allred Reading Placement Inventory*. Oklahoma City, Oklahoma: The Economy Company.

The Primary Language Record. (1988) London, England: Center for Language in Primary Education. (Also published by Heinemann Educational Books, Portsmouth, New Hampshire.)

Study Skills, Pre-Reading Strategies, Before, During & After Reading Strategies, Expository and Narrative Text Structure

Atwell, Nancy. (1990) *Coming to Know*. Portsmouth, New Hampshire: Boynton/Cook Publishers.

Graves, M. F., Juel, C. & Graves, B.B. (1998) *Teaching Reading in the 21st Century*. Needham Heights, Massachusetts: Allyn & Bacon.

Lapp, Diane, Flood, James, & Farnan, Nancy. (Eds.) (1996) *Content Area Reading and A Learning: Instructional Strategies* (Second Edition) Needham Heights, Massachusetts: Allyn & Bacon.

Robinson, R.P. (1941) *Effective Study*. New York: Harper & Row.

Vacca, Richard T., & Vacca, Joanne L. (1993) *Content Area Reading* (Fourth Edition) New York: HarperCollins.

Yopp, Ruth Helen & Yopp, Hallie Kay. (1992) *Literature-Based Reading Activities*. Needham Heights, Massachusetts: Allyn & Bacon.

English As Second Language

Peregoy, S. & Boyle, O. (1997) *Reading, Writing, and Learning in ESL: A Resource Book for K-12 Teachers*. White Plains, New York: Longman.

Richard-Amato, Patricia A. & Snow, Marguerite Ann. (1992) *The Multicultural Classroom: Readings for Content Area Teachers*. Reading, Massachusetts: Addison-Wesley Publishing Company.

Literature Circles

Blatt, Gloria, T. Ed. (1993) *Once Upon a Folk Tale: Capturing the Folklore Process with Children*. New York, New York: Teachers College Press.

Bosma, Bette. (1992) *Fairy Tales, Fables, Legends, and Myths: Using Folk Literature in Your Classroom*. New York, New York: Teachers College Press.

Daniels, H. (1994). *Literature Circles: Voice and Choice in the Student-Centered Classroom*. York, Maine: Stenhouse Publishers

Moss, Joy F. (1992). *Focus on Literature: A Context for Literacy Learning*. Katonah, New York: Richard C. Owen Publishers, Inc.

Samway, K. Davies, & Whang, G. (1996) *Literature Study Circles in a Multicultural Classroom*. York, Maine: Stenhouse Publishers

Smith, K. (1990) Entertaining a Text: A Reciprocal Process. In *Talking about Books: Creating Literate Communities*. K.G. Short & K.M. Pierce (Eds.) Portsmouth, New Hampshire: Heinemann.

Spelling, Vocabulary

Clymer, Theodore L. (1963) The Utility of Phonics Generalizations in the Primary Grades. *The Reading Teacher*. 16: 252-58.

Cunningham, P. M. (1995) *Phonics They Use: Words for Reading and Writing* (Second Edition). New York: HarperCollins.

Henderson, Edmund H. & Bears, James. (1980) *Developmental and Cognitive Aspects of Learning to Spell*. Newark, Delaware. International Reading Association.

Richek, M. A., Schudt Caldwell, J., Holt Jennings, J. & Lerner, J.W. (1996) *Reading Problems: Assessment and Teaching Strategies*. Needham Heights, Massachusetts: Allyn & Bacon.

The titles that are starred* in the list of references are textbooks that cover in-depth all components of reading.

Master List of Terms

Anecdotal Records
Assessment
    running records
    miscue analysis
    informal reading inventories
Baseline information
Before, During, After (Into, Through, Beyond)
Benchmarks & Developmental Milestones
    observational checklist
Cloze Procedure
Comprehension
    Literal
    Main idea
    Comparison
    Analytical
    Cause & effect
    Drawing conclusions
    Generalizations
    Evaluation
Comprehension Strategies
    Self-monitoring
    Self-correcting
    Rereading
    Note taking
    Outlining
    Summarizing
Concepts of Print
Conferences
Cue Systems
Decodable Text & Predictable Test
Environmental Print
Expository Text Structure

Guided Reading
Interactive Writing
Language Experience Approach
Learning logs
Listening Samples
Literature Circles
Mapping
Narrative Text Structure
Observations
Onsets & Rimes
Oral Cloze
Oral Language Development
Phonemic Awareness
Phonics and Systematic Phonics
Instruction
Portfolios
Prereading Strategies
Readers theatre
Reciprocal Teaching
Retelling
Shared Reading
Study Skill Strategies
    Graphic Organizers
    KWL
    SQ3R
Think-aloud
(VAKT)Visual/Auditory/Kinesthetic/Tactile)
    techniques
Vocabulary
Word Analysis
Word Walls